A CREATIVE LOOK at LIFE

Issues—Questions—Answers

by
D. S. Spears, Ed. D.

WESTBOW
PRESS®
A DIVISION OF THOMAS NELSON
& ZONDERVAN

WestBow Press
A Division of Thomas Nelson & Zondervan
1663 Liberty Drive
Bloomington, IN 47403
www.westbowpress.com
1 (866) 928-1240

ISBN: 978-1-4908-9890-2 (sc)
ISBN: 978-1-4908-9892-6 (hc)
ISBN: 978-1-4908-9891-9 (e)

WestBow Press rev. date: 08/19/2017

To the youth, young adults,
and all others earnestly seeking truth.

Contents

Illustrations and Graphics by D.S. Spears

Part A

Part B

Poetry by D. S. Spears

Part A

Part B

Acknowledgments

Most importantly, I acknowledge the Triune God of the Bible: the Father, the Word and the Holy Spirit as my inspiration. It is a privilege to offer this book to His glory and to bring truth to truth-starved generations.

Some very special people deserve recognition for their precious friendship, support, and encouragement. A grateful "thank-you" to:

—Friends and prayer partners, Luther and Betty Foster. Betty, a former U. S. Government Analyst document editor, intensely combed the first draft for errors and offered suggestions for phrasing.

—My wonderful husband, H. Truman Spears, who keeps me laughing, often raises issues for deep thought, and tolerated the time required to produce this work;

—Every student's blessing through lessons learned about how best to teach and for their love;

—The many individuals who have influenced me for the Lord; I am confident God keeps track of their rewards.

IN LOVING MEMORY:

—A dear friend since high school, Verleen Jeanette (Calle) Mackey, a former English teacher who, in the midst of a serious health challenge, volunteered her valuable time and energy editing for errors and format anomalies and suggested changes for clarification.

—Kay Solomon, a dear friend and prayer partner for sixteen years, continued her prayer support despite difficult personal and health issues.

Both will remain in my heart even after I see them again in heaven.

Preface

A Creative Look at Life: Issues—Questions—Answers © is a new title for a previously published book: *Who, What, Where, When, Why and How? A Creative Look at Life's Main Issues* ©, 2014.

Four reasons for this republication are:

1. the unwieldiness of the first title,
2. to create a title closely related to the sequel in progress,
3. to correct a few overlooked typographical errors (entirely my fault),
4. to repaginate some illustrations.

The first book was transferred from the original publisher to Westbow Press, a division of Thomas Nelson and Zondervan, Inc., allowing this opportunity to make these improvements. I gratefully thank them.

Comments on the first publication:

June 1, 2014 -- "I really enjoyed and learned and laughed and was enlightened all at the same time! What more could I ask for?"—G. on Facebook.

"I loved it! It is a book you will want in your library. I highly recommend it to all." Gerry on Amazon.com

June 9, 2014 – "Diane, I am very impressed by your new book. I am in awe of anyone who has the imagination and skills to put together something like this. The stories are imaginative and well done. I think the book would be an excellent text for Sunday school classes for young people."—Lee by email.

Introduction

What You Will Find

Both A and B parts of *A Creative Look at Life* © uniquely address the most commonly asked life questions and issues, designed to prompt higher thinking processes than many of us are regularly confronted with in daily life. Part B, "Forest Primeval" continues the format with another important introduction and five chapters of a long allegory that highlight current cultural issues everyone should understand. A subsequent publication, *Looking Deeper at Life: Issues—Questions—Answers* ©, will follow to provide expanded material to these prevailing life issues.

The Format

Every chapter begins with an original proverb, then presents illustrated parables, anecdotes acting as parables, allegories, short stories, poetry, comments or a combination thereof, related to the theme. Each chapter concludes with the old phrase: "Moral of the Story" like the famous *Aesop's Fables*. The dictionary definitions [1] for important words are as follows:

— *proverb*: a brief popular saying that gives advice about how people should live or that expresses a belief that is generally thought to be true; a maxim . . .
— *parable*: a short fictitious story that teaches a moral lesson, a universal truth, or religious principle
— *allegory*: the expression by means of symbolic fictional figures and actions of truths or generalizations about human

---

1. By permission. From *Merriam-Webster's Collegiate® Dictionary, 11th Edition* ©2015 by Merriam-Webster, Inc. (www.Merriam-Webster.com).

existence; also: an instance (as in a story or painting) of such expression
— *anecdote*: a short, true account or story of an interesting event that can act like a parable
— *moral of the story*: a lesson that is learned from a story or an experience

All Scripture references are from the New King James Version (NKJV) of the Bible unless identified otherwise.

Why Metaphors?

Metaphors, similes, symbols and analogies focus our attention on truths and wisdom to compare life experiences with spiritual matters and are word illustrations that "draw" mental pictures. Serious ideas and issues are presented in an entertaining and memorable format to ease information digestion. Metaphors and such prompt and guide deeper critical thinking about important issues concerning our existence now and after life is completed on this beautiful and important blue planet, a comparatively minute speck in vast dark space.

Allegory versus Literal

Keep your mind and heart open to Bible stories such as "Noah and the Ark," "Jonah and the Big Fish," "Adam and Eve" and more as not allegorical but as true historical events recorded to teach valuable lessons. God has infinite resources for unique, creative and often startling methods to catch our attention to important issues. The Old Testament presents many examples in which people needed to experience attention-getting circumstances to make the lessons stick. Observation is the wisest way to learn, but most of us still learn best by experience. Some concepts, statements and scriptures will be repeated for emphasis because repetition is a proved learning method.

I believe you will enjoy this adventure.

Metaphor

A metaphor grabs and holds attention
To embed an exquisite thought or value.
The simile stirs a unique vision,
A mind map with a novel view—
While speaking a thousand words
In silence, wonder and awe.
Deeply sensed nouns, adjectives and verbs
From A to Z, from *aleph* to *tau*,
Emerge from silence to audible expression
Provoking new concepts to face
How this inner comprehension
Challenges thinkers to reject or embrace.

Diane Shields Spears ©

A Creative Look at Life
Part A

Beginning of Spring ©

To All Truth Seekers

• •

Life is like a pineapple. It's a challenge getting to the good part.

• •

Most Important

If you make a list of the most important questions you want answered before you die, what would you ask first? Take time with this before proceeding to prompt your thinking in the right direction. Are your questions about temporary issues of earthly living, eternal issues or both?

Now compare your list with the most commonly asked life questions listed below. If you made a list, does the following set prompt you to add more?

1. Who am I?
2. Where did I come from?
3. Why am I here?
4. What is truth? Where do I find it?
5. How do I know God is real?
6. Why is there evil in the world?
7. Why Jesus?
8. Can I control events in my life?
9. How should I live?
10. What happens after life on Earth?

More Questions

1. Do you have answers to the above questions? How do you know they are right?
2. Suppose your answers were challenged (for example by torture or threat of death), would you stand or falter?

Tuning Out and Turning Off

If you have been disillusioned by empty religious practices, join the growing segment who is questioning established religions and denominationalism of all sorts, prompted partly by observing hypocrisy in those who adhere to them and partly by numerous opposing beliefs.

Religions, multiple denominations thereof, secular and political philosophies attempt to provide answers, but present confusing and obvious illogical conclusions, are completely wrong, or have partial truth. Only a few seem on the mark. Most fail to give satisfactory answers, and many people have departed from believing God can be known. Organized religions have been packaged in many lovely wraps and ribbons, yet are empty or confusing with conflicting information and subjective opinions. The result—the truth about God in public life is now illusive with secularism, humanism, pantheism and more creeping into the void created by abandoning authentic Christian heritage. This book does not promote religion as the term is widely understood. Instead, it clarifies issues that interfere with comprehending truth, suggests answers to very difficult issues and emphasizes what a relationship with God can become.

Ask Your Own Questions.

You are asked to question everything you read in other sources and everything you read here. Be careful about dismissing ideas until you have conducted your personal investigation using trustworthy sources for absolute truth.

Absolute truth contains ideas and beliefs that apply to all people and situations. Subjective truth contains ideas and beliefs that are not applicable to all people. The striking difference between absolute and subjective truth will become clear as you read this book and the sequel.

Go Deep!

Try writing a profound answer to each question in the above list and expand each category with your questions. Keeping a journal of your thoughts while reading is recommended for the greatest benefit.

Are you honestly satisfied with the answers you have? Question everything with an open mind and with a willingness to change your opinions and beliefs, if necessary. If something continues to elude you, research it thoroughly.

Sometimes placing a mystery "on the shelf" for a while will allow the answer to come from an unexpected source, such as a friend, a book, a dream, prayer or when you are occupied with something much less important or perhaps entirely unrelated.

Understanding Your Purpose

Making life count and understanding your purpose requires learning some valuable lessons while looking for truth in circumstances and information. We are foolish if we fail to learn something from all we encounter. Even if we recognize error, we have learned. An alert: our faulty base of *incomplete* knowledge and experience puts us in the danger zone of wrong conclusions.

Answers to life issues suggested here are not given in the order of the above list. Some parables contain many lessons to inspire a life-long personal search for truth, understanding a relationship with God and why you are here on this planet. If you already know your purpose for your earthly existence and for eternity—great! Just remember learning more truth is always available.

Finding and embracing truth is possible without understanding its depths, because truth is both an intellectual and a heart issue. Believing with your whole heart you have found truth is not the destination. Continue searching for your purpose for being on this Earth and then living it out with joy.

Additional extensive concepts addressing the above list of questions will be provided in the future sequel with deeper challenges to stimulate critical thinking. Prepare absorption of that deeper content with this book.

Sincerity

The majority think they find meaning for life in various religious experiences and are 100 percent sincere in their search and findings. Caution! It is possible to believe wholeheartedly in something that is right and possible to wholeheartedly believe in something containing error. We can be sincere, but sincerely wrong. Question everything. God is never offended by honest and earnest queries. In fact, asking questions will rescue you from boredom and emptiness and launch an exciting adventure toward truth. God will provide answers in His timing. He has and is the answer to every question.

Heads Up

Take time with the Scripture references in the text. I respectfully request that you not dismiss the ideas and information given without serious consideration. We can all learn something from anyone and anything, even if we think it is negative or of little to no value. The Bible is at the least considered by scholars to be important literature even if its truth is not recognized.

Some Scripture verses have more than one application and are intentionally repeated, partly for its application to new thoughts, partly for emphasis and partly because of its strategical success in permanent retention, firmly embedding these truths into spirits and souls. We humans need to read, hear and speak the Word of God often because the enemy will cause confusion and forgetfulness at every opportunity. Repetition also builds faith that is an effective weapon against Satan's attacks of doubt.

Valuable Resources

If you need a Bible, the New King James (NKJV) is updated from the Old English and clarifies some of the difficult words and passages from the original languages of Hebrew and Greek. Many English words have totally changed meanings from the time the King James Version (KJV) was published in A.D. 1611.

Several easy-to-use web sites provide all available versions with the feature of side-by-side comparisons. Also recommended is a hard copy of the Bible for your lap while you sit in a comfortable chair with your feet propped up. If you are serious about studying the Word of God, you will need the KJV and *Strong's Exhaustive Concordance of the Bible* that is calibrated to the KJV. It lists all words, the original languages, the definitions and the locations in Scripture. The NKJV is used in this book unless otherwise stated.

God's Word is truth and life (John 6:63) plus transformation power! Paraphrases (restatements, not translations) make the content easier but the original Word of God, not paraphrasing, packs the spiritual table with nutritious food for the spirit and soul. The Bible is *inerrant* in its original languages (Hebrew, Greek, and some Aramaic). You can trust the message.

Take the Challenge.

Prepare yourself to consider challenges of ideas, information and suppositions that may contradict what you have thought or have been taught. All possibilities should be honestly considered and compared with Scripture and with no preconceived agenda—the only strategy to make informed decisions. The study should prompt your thinking on a deeper level about eternal issues than you perhaps have ever thought before.

Take your time with this information. The content of this book is enjoyable in addition to being a thought-provoking and memorable experience. Engage your mind in this adventure.

Question for Thought:

How does the proverb at the beginning of this chapter apply to you?

••• 2 •••
Who Cares?

••••••••••••••••••••••••••••••
Your existence is important to someone.
••••••••••••••••••••••••••••••

Peach's sparse pinkish-tan feathers allowed her yellow skin to peek through, giving her the distinct appearance of peach fuzz, making her noticeable among her siblings, Porter, Percy, Portia, Petunia and Pansy that were fading yellow. Father Rooster and Mother Hen were astonished when Peach hatched and worried that they had a disabled toddler. Even though Peach was the youngest, she was larger than her siblings and clumsy too, giving Mother Hen more worries and need for watchfulness and discipline, because the sisters made fun of her awkwardness and appearance.

When each chick was a week old, Mother Hen introduced them to the fenced pen where they had a grand time pecking the weeds for bugs. Peach constantly tripped over her own feet. Mother Hen kept a careful eye on her making certain that she ate enough and was not injured from falling. Porter and Percy partially watched out for Peach but were distracted by good bug pecking and hung out mostly with Father Rooster. Portia, Petunia and Pansy were jealous of the extra attention Peach received from Mother Hen and would at times keep Peach away from the best bug areas. All especially loved the good eating miraculously appearing each morning in the air over their heads, falling into a pan and onto the ground.

Peach was precocious and curious about many things and was the first to ask, "Mother, why are there so many different bugs?"

"I'm not sure, dear," was her reply.

"Why do these bugs jump?" Mother Hen was silent, because Peach was excitedly cheeping as she chased a grasshopper.

"Mother, what's this new food that comes from the sky and doesn't move?"

"I'm not sure, dear."

"Mother, where does this different food come from?"

Mother Hen's answer about the Source was also vague, but she knew it was good. Father Rooster had no opinion. The Source always provided seed and water, replenished the straw and checked the nest for enemies. Mother Hen will always remember a very frightening experience. A long slender creature with scary eyes and no feet stole one of her eggs. Her alarmed clucking brought the Source who located the creature and dispatched it quickly.

At first, the sight of the Source's interesting but strange, thick wings frightened Mother Hen. She knew they were not legs and feet, and were without feathers, only interesting lines and colors. They were able to do things her wings could not do. Then she began to realize they must be very special wing-hands. She had no clue about how she knew mysteries. She just did. She knew the animal next door was a goat with four feet instead of two. The feet did not resemble hers at all, but she simply knew they were feet. The goat made strange sounds but was not scary after the first time she heard it. The cow was huge and always made scary sounds. Mother Hen shared her knowledge with the chicks.

Peach was the only one curious about but not afraid of the different noises these creatures made. She particularly liked the sound of the ducks that made her laugh. She even tried imitating them to everyone's joy. "Mother, what are these? I like them!" She loved Father Rooster's crowing, which she also tried to imitate.

The Source also made sounds from higher in the air than they could see but were strangely comforting. It also had large things that moved like feet and were hard like the cow's hooves but were completely different from the feet of other animals and there were only two of them. The hoof-like things also had long worms on them. Mother Hen had tried pecking those, but they were tough, would not separate from the feet and were definitely not food. The Source was a mystery. She cautioned her tiny chicks to avoid the large hoof-like feet.

A sustained storm with lightning, thunder and several inches of rain caused the chicks to shiver with fear. Mother Hen gathered them under her wings on the nest while Father Rooster rested on a shelf above as if guarding them. When the storm was over, the chicks all hopped onto the ground landing in mud puddles, delighted to be playing in the sunshine. They soon discovered the great fun of mud baths and slinging the sticky stuff on each other.

"These are not worms!"

"Hey, Percy, look!" as Porter flung mud on him raising quite a ruckus. The mud began clinging to their feathers weighing them down, unable to extract themselves from it. Father Rooster stood immobilized at a distance with confusion and helplessness. Peach, partly because of her size advantage and sparse feathers, was able to shake free. She found some high ground already mostly solid, picked her way to Portia, Petunia and Pansy to help, but the mud was drying quickly on their feathers from the hot sun. Porter and Percy emphatically stated they could manage.

"Motherrrrrrr!" peeped Peach as loudly as she could.

Mother Hen began clucking an alarm. Suddenly, the Source, who was already on his way to investigate their welfare after the storm, appeared emitting an almost deafening, deep laugh that made them shiver with momentary fright. With its great, capable wing-hands, the Source lifted each chick gently from the mud and placed it in a pan of shallow water. His voice was soothing and musical. Portia, Petunia and Pansy began to giggle as water was scooped over them, softening the mud. Porter and Percy peeped and splashed with delight as soon as their wings were unstuck from their sides.

Peach was the last to be placed in the bath. The mysterious wing-hands removed the chicks from the bath, placed them on a soft cloth and patted

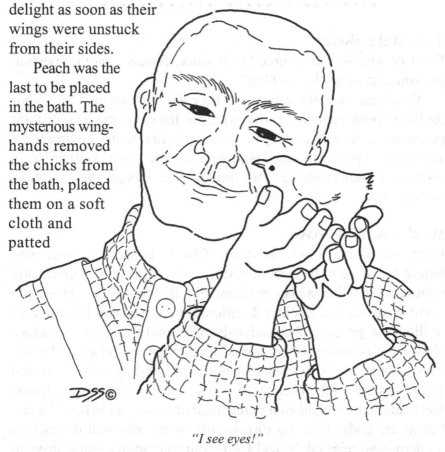

"I see eyes!"

each one until they were no longer dripping. Mother Hen continued her concerned but soft clucking as Peach's five siblings were carefully placed in her nest. Father Rooster unfroze and ran to investigate. Mother Hen watched nervously as the Source lifted Peach higher in the air where she saw for the first time what she knew were eyes. The Source caressed Peach's cheek and thanked her for her brave attempts to rescue her siblings. He then placed her gently in the nest with Mother Hen, who folded them all under her wings and continued clucking softly at the Source, feeling quite inadequate to express her gratitude. They felt safe. All the chicks peeped at the Source and thanked Peach too. Peach was awestruck and declared that the Source was not just good but "really good." Father Rooster strutted and crowed his best crow.

• •

The Metaphors

What or who is your source? Is it work, fortune, another person, government, yourself—or God?

Chickens are bird-brained, so they are a reasonable metaphor for limited understanding and interpreting the environment with their perspective. Actually, everyone interprets his or her environment according to personal understanding and experience. Mother Hen's instinctive knowledge was still limited even though she just knew some things.

Modern Thinking

Every person has a built-in sense of God's existence. Those who ignore it choose to be boss of self in adhering to philosophies and ethics related to humanism that humanity is autonomous. It has been silently woven into public educational directives and has affected millions of people subconsciously, ignorantly and by conscious choice. Self-awareness programs, meditation exercises and more have been instituted to teach techniques of building self-esteem and self as supreme. After decades of exposure to this philosophy, it now feels natural to a significant percentage of society to believe human beings are gods. Thus, no surprise that many who call themselves modern have rejected the real God—our true Source—and strive to eliminate all references to God in national life.

The Humanist Manifesto appeals to humanity's ego, thereby accounting for its attraction and influence. Just enough common sense and truth about using your abilities to be the best you can be deceives the uninformed into thinking it might be the way. The

Humanist Manifesto declares self is humanity's source, and the Bible states emphatically that God is our Source, and that He is not just good, but to quote Peach, *"really good."*

Search Light

You are encouraged to investigate your true Source's ID by reading the Bible while turning the searchlight honestly on your own heart. If you are unfamiliar with the Bible, you will begin to see your need for a Source much greater than yourself, and you will be informed of Scripture's actual contents. Secular scholars who deny the Bible as truth consider it as important literature and might recommend reading it just for information to enable informed discussion.

The Bible will not be overwhelming if you begin reading in the Gospel of John (fourth book in the New Testament). Then back up to the beginning of the New Testament and proceed from there. Then read the book of Genesis, the first book of the Old Testament.

Moral Of The Story

— *Practical lesson:* Find the Source who cares the most.
— *Spiritual lesson:* Learn continually about your real Source.

What other lessons might be contained in this parable?

Lollie Pop

•••••••••••••••••••••••••••••••
Learn from the great and the small.
•••••••••••••••••••••••••••••••

Many years ago, we were blessed to find a beautiful English pointer pup on the roadside. Someone had dumped her with an open can of dog food, and she had eaten down as far as her little tongue could reach. She was so hungry that she ate all we could feed her— so much so that we commented, grinning, she might pop, the inspiration for her name. She was a delight and a surprise her entire life.

Lollie was the most obedient and smartest dog we ever owned. Our house was on a busy street with no fence. She learned the property boundary when my husband, Truman, trained her with an emphatic "No!" while standing at the end of the driveway as cars zoomed past in both directions. She also understood our

Abandoned

older brown mixed breed dog, Dutch Chocolate, needing a companion. She shared her doghouse with him, even though he had a nice one of his own. Both climbing into and arranging themselves in a doghouse made for one was amazing and amusing.

Lollie had a weakness—her only repeated disobedience. She would raid the trashcan in the open carport if something very fragrant beckoned her. One of our sons would unthinkingly throw a food wrapper in the trashcan on his way from his car to the house, and Lollie would sniff it, tip the can, scatter the contents and shred the wrapper. She was constantly chastised for it, but the temptation was too great. Her nose always won.

One day Lollie did not greet us as usual when we arrived home. We called. Walking through the carport toward the house, we saw her hugging the house and slithering around the corner trying to get to her doghouse undetected. Her crime—the trash had been raided. We laughed heartily. She was the perfect living example of Proverbs 28:1 that states the guilty flee when no one pursues—conviction and hiding before detection and inevitable consequences.

Lollie entertained herself by chasing, not butterflies, but their shadows at home and by pursuing sea gulls on the beach. At first, we tied her to the truck bumper at the beach, not knowing what her behavior would be among so many other folks but soon realized worrying was unwarranted. The parading, swooping and squabbling gulls teased her hunter heritage. The intensity of her focus, quivering muscles and controlled squeaks emitting from her throat spoke volumes. We assessed gulls would be able to fly above her, were not in danger and would probably not attack her, so we turned her loose.

Squealing with excitement, she immediately charged after the gulls at high speed parallel with the surf. We had not walked with her and told her "No!" at a certain distance so she would recognize a boundary. When she got far enough we called and called until we realized she could not hear us over the surf roar. Truman had the motorcycle ready just in case and pursued. She was obviously confused and tried to find us among the people near her, but when she saw Truman approaching, joy and relief actually showed on her countenance.

Her action was not disobedience because we had not given her beach boundary instruction. She followed Truman back and rested with us for a few moments, before taking off again. Truman walked toward the motorcycle, but she suddenly turned as if on wheels at about fifty yards and raced back past us in the opposite direction. She stopped about the same distance as before as if she had a built-in fifty-yard odometer and a U-turn sign. She spun around and repeated the whole process several times until she flopped in the sand by the truck panting hard. Amazingly, she also seemed to understand a safety boundary at the beach.

Sensing her gull-chasing strategy needed perfecting, she began crouching like a stalking cat. Once, she spied a small moving object a short distance down the beach. She began her sneak, lifting each foot with remarkable concentration like a super slow motion movie, taking nearly five minutes to reach the object. Other people began to watch with fascination. Finally getting close, she pounced, only to discover a black plastic bag partially buried in the sand, edges waving with the breeze. Many spectators laughed, and on returning, her facial expression and slinking posture screamed embarrassment. She hid under the truck for a while. Many other incidents with Lollie gave us great pleasure.

Unfortunately, she contracted heartworms during the time when these destructive creatures began spreading in Texas. The vet treated her, but her heart was damaged and her activities had to tone down. When we took her to the beach, we wondered how we would discourage gull chasing, so we tied her to the truck bumper. Surprisingly, she ignored the gulls, seeming to understand her limitations. We determined it would be safe to turn her loose, expecting her to enjoy sniffing the

Lollie Contented

the fishiness of the driftwood, sand, shells and seaweed. Instead, she turned her attention to the jumping mullet in the surf and allowed the waves to move and support her weight as she lunged after them, entertaining herself. She seemed unconcerned about not catching one. Lollie's adapted behavior demonstrated the scripture that admonishes us to be content in every circumstance (Philippians 4:11b).

I learned from Lollie. The vet could not totally correct her condition and she could have moped around looking pitiful. She simply changed her focus and appeared perfectly content. It was a healthy change for her, a delight for us, and she lived longer than predicted. I believe Lollie was a gift to us as a beautiful example and a great pleasure. What a blessing!

• •

Contentment versus Frustration

If only we could be as content as Lollie was in whatever conditions we find ourselves. I have given myself pity parties from time-to-time over things I cannot change, do not yet know how to change or am waiting for a change. I learned that self-pity is not healthy, because it leads to dark places of the mind and emotions. I remind myself that the Lord is in charge of my life, so I have every reason to be content.

Have you ever had a frustration fit over thwarted plans and/or malfunctioning contraptions? Mechanical breakdowns, unnecessary delays, unexpected changed circumstances and such can provoke intense reactions. Did you respond positively or react negatively? Anger? Stress? Worry? Fear? Hopelessness? Contentment in some circumstances might seem impossible.

Frustrations from an outside source are often beyond anyone's control and definitely provoke emotional, mental and physical effects even if not felt immediately or intensely. Frustration can lead to fear, worry and/or anger that unfavorable situations will escalate and remain that way. A high level of continued stress has been scientifically linked to arthritis, cancer, heart conditions, diabetes and more.

Hopelessness, if not relieved, seems to be the main culprit in the downward spiral to clinical depression. Deferred hope means taking a long time for the reward and makes the "heart sick" (Proverbs 13:12). Many succumb to the ever-present temptation to give up, but quitting can easily progress from withdrawal to the belief that nobody cares.

Dealing With the Negative

The answer to dealing successfully with undesirable situations is in God's Word. He thoroughly understands the difficulty of receiving help when oppression, depression, unmanageable emotions and intolerable circumstances reign. He gives an important strategy—meditate on ("mutter") His Word by choosing verses that address specific situations with God's promise of deliverance. Speak them repeatedly until they lodge in your heart and build faith. Put the verses in your mouth and let your ears hear it. This is powerful ammunition for the battle of the mind—a repeated theme in this book. Changing habitual mind-sets of self-pity, hopelessness or thinking we are not important can be difficult. Friends who try to help can offer comfort and sympathy, but only Scripture—the Word of God—has power to deliver from despair while giving hope during the turmoil.

Status Quo or Change?

Lollie could not do what she loved. She changed her focus and appeared to be content with her limitations and even loving her new pursuit. We should never just accept the status quo or give up—Lollie did what she could. However, we are not to "beat our heads against the wall" in fighting what we absolutely cannot change. A way is always available to be content in whatever situations we find ourselves until things improve. The key: give every detail to the Lord with praise and worship, not necessarily *for* every circumstance but *in* (during) every circumstance (1 Thessalonians 5:18). Give it all to Him to make the best changes. God can do anything! He can convert anything negative to a positive outcome (Romans 8:28). When we surrender all our burdens to the Lord, He teaches us through them, and in the end, we will know why we must praise Him *in* and *for* all things.

Unconditional Love

Scripture repeatedly emphasizes God's love for us but can sound trite if delivered as a final solution without any real supporting evidence, as if just the statement itself cures all. "God loves you" is not as powerful as the following scripture:

> 16 For God so loved the world that He gave His only begotten Son, that whoever believes in Him should not perish but have everlasting life.
> 17 For God did not send His Son into the world to condemn the world, but that the world through Him might be saved (John 3:16-17).

Regardless of its familiarity, the statement "God loves you" is true and is an important one to hear often. Follow the statement with the above verses and other supporting scriptures. We may need to hear it and read it a thousand times to actually receive it, because we are so self-help oriented.

In addition, perhaps your background has programmed you to think you are unlovable. Being fully persuaded that God loves you *unconditionally* will be the Rock to stand on. That Rock elevates our metaphorical feet above what appears to be a disastrous flood intended to destroy. The Lord and His Word are the power to deliver from negative physical, mental and emotional circumstances that no other source can do.

Moral Of The Story

— *Practical lesson:* Let animals teach valuable lessons.
— *Spiritual lesson:* Let the knowledge that God will help you change what you can and to be content in any circumstances you absolutely cannot change.

What other lessons might be contained in this anecdote?

... 4 ...

The Knothole Gang and Friends

•••••••••••••••••••••••••••••

Nature is not to be worshiped.
It is one of our teachers.

•••••••••••••••••••••••••••

A large dining area window faces a birdbath, feeders and watering pan, rewarding us with entertaining views of wildlife varieties and their relationships with each other. Visitors include squirrels, birds, raccoons, deer, feral cats prowling for birds, neighbors' fugitive dogs occasionally escaping their pens and the one time nanny goat wearing a bell that climbed my art studio porch steps to stare at me through the sliding glass door.

The Trap

After our home was built, we added a full-length eight-by-forty-four foot screened porch, and when no mosquitoes appeared, we left one end unscreened. This opening became the entrance to a wildlife trap. Numerous birds forgot how they found themselves pushing against the screen at the far end, some with claws and beaks caught.

Most were easy to rescue, but white wing doves panicked, beating their wings against the screen when we gently put both hands around them. A woodpecker emitted squawking protests at higher decibels than normal as he was being carried to the open end of the porch. A roadrunner was evidently contemplating how to get through the screen at the closed end while quietly sitting on the edge of a table between the screen and a huge draping night blooming cereus. Truman overcame his hesitation about how hard the roadrunner might peck and inched toward him attempting a capture. Mr. Roadrunner spied him, jumped from the table to a position aiming his attention toward the unscreened opening. He immediately made tracks with feet whirling the full length of the porch. Surprisingly, the hummingbirds remained perfectly still while extracting beaks and claws from the screen, cooperating 100 percent. What an awesome experience to hold a hummingbird loosely cupped in my hands! None of our captives were injured in the delicate rescuing process.

After a few years, the screen was so stretched by the north wind and tears from claws and beaks that we removed it. We had not realized how much the screen had dimmed our view of the lake, but we missed the little dramas of trapped creatures.

The Knothole Gang—

A Spanish oak tree with three holes in the trunk near our porch was a favorite for woodpeckers and squirrels. The top hole housed a woodpecker family with new hatchlings, a fat mama squirrel and her three tiny "squirrel-ettes" occupied the largest middle hole, and we observed no activity in the smallest bottom hole. The baby woodies could be heard occasionally but had not been seen, nor had we noticed squirrels and woodpeckers simultaneously on that oak trunk.

One day, Mama Squirrel and her three were clearly enjoying chasing each other on the trunk, racing up, down and around. Mama must have said it was nap time, because the babies crawled into the hole. They may not have arranged themselves to leave room for mom, because when she tried to enter, it appeared she did not fit and her hind half was still outside the hole. She began to simply relax in that position, letting her legs dangle, probably while the babies squirmed or continued to play inside. Mrs. Woody happened to spy Mama Squirrel's posture and must have thought her baby woodies were in jeopardy. Mrs. Woody dive-bombed Mrs. Squirrel and pecked her rear end. Mama Squirrel suddenly found room with her kids.

The result of this little drama was that both families changed addresses. The relocation of the squirrel-ettes was most interesting. They were apparently not yet experienced in tree acrobatics, because Mama Squirrel led each one separately down the trunk, across the dangerous ground to a nearby tree and secured them in the thick foliage higher than their original hole. We missed the relocation of the woodpecker family.

—And Friends

The deer provide great pleasure. We name the regular, identifiable visitors according to appearance and behavior. Camel was a doe with a loose lower lip and slightly buggy eyes, the Pinhead Brothers had noticeably narrow heads, and Pretty Boy was a twelve-point buck so large and impressive with a square jaw and heavier muscles that I stated, "He's the athlete of the deer families." The deer might love their names if only they knew. Several doe and one beautiful buck with perfect eight points will eat from our hands—the training by our neighbor who is also a softy about animals.

More Drama

One event dramatically stands out. An ailing doe brought her infant spotted twins and settled them under the birdbath in the shade. She was sick and tried repeatedly to drink from the birdbath but was only able to wave her nose across the water in obvious distress. She did this for several hours and walked away. We wondered if she was looking for a place to die, so we looked diligently and found her reclining under my art studio in the darkest, furthest corner. She had entered where the skirting had been removed for water pipe repair and had not been replaced. We removed some skirting on the other side to force her out by turning the water hose on her. It seemed cruel but was necessary that she not die under there and then have one hundred times the difficulty removing her body. Both openings were quickly blocked. She did not return to her twins. We found her about two hours later where she had laid down for the last time only thirty feet from our front door. We had to rope and drag her with the truck uphill to "the woods" far enough on our property so decomposition could not be detected, hoping rather morbidly that the buzzards would help.

Obviously, the doe expected us to care for her fawns. We were unprepared and had no way of knowing if they would be ready for solid food. They cautiously investigated a small pan of milk and drank, then nibbled bits of whole wheat bread. By this time dark was coming, and we prayed that they find a safe place to spend the night. We think they crawled under the porch, because they reappeared at first light.

The orphaned twins hung around our front steps for a few days before exploring. They always traveled together, and came for predicted three meals a day of bread, water, whatever vegetable cuttings we happened to have and for special young deer pellets purchased at the first chance. One fawn, noticeably smaller and thinner than the other, never seemed to gain weight or show any growth, even though they both ate heartily. I named them Bitsie and Bigger Bits, but Truman changed Bigger Bits to Ben,

Bitsie and Bigger Bits (Ben)

despite my protests that he might not be a buck, and we would have to change his name to Benita. I stuck with Bigger Bits for a while, insisting that it was cuter but reluctantly acquiesced.

Bitsie and Ben became almost pets. I was concerned they would become too tame, possibly making them vulnerable around hunters or poachers. Feeding and enjoying them carried on for about three weeks before we saw them trying to merge with another group of doe and fawns. Bitsie and Ben stood out, because they were born later in the summer, were smaller and disadvantaged by not nursing long enough. Other doe would not let them nurse, and other doe's jealous fawns blocked them.

One afternoon while watching this group, Bitsie tried again to nurse on the nearest doe. That doe's larger fawn stood on his hind legs and began walloping Bitsie with his front hooves, knocking her down. Ben instantly sprang into action in defense of his sister and returned the wallops. The bigger fawn ran under our fig tree. Ben went to the opposite side of the fig tree and stared him down, making the bigger fawn back up. Ben advanced a couple of steps, stomped a hoof and looked ready to continue the issue. Suddenly, the bigger fawn decided Ben was serious, ran to his mom kicking up dust and immediately began nursing. It reminded me of a child running to hide behind mom's skirt. We laughed heartily. Bitsie was OK, but no doe would allow the orphans to nurse.

Hazards of the Wild

The deer have trained us to watch for them. One day we heard a repeated clunk, clunk with each step on our terraced walkway. A piece of very old (perhaps antique) rusty can was wedged in Ben's left front hoof. We longed to help. He was not limping and did not appear to be in pain, but he did bite at it occasionally, revealing his annoyance. It was lodged firmly. After clunking around for four or five more days, the piece of rusty can had dislodged and he was back to normal.

Be Prepared.

If you love animals, be prepared for the occasional tragedy. When the twins were probably three months old, Bitsie did not come with Ben for two days in a row. Our neighbor saw the carcass of a tiny fawn on the road below us. Swirling buzzards were spotted the day before, and we worried that it was Bitsie. She never showed again, so we had to assume the negative. Ben continued coming for an occasional handout. He was growing, but had not caught up in size with the other fawns, so he was still identifiable.

The following spring, tiny bumps on his head promised antlers, so he keeps his name. He still visited us irregularly for pellets and became a handsome eleven-pointer in his fourth year. As of this writing, we have not seen him since mating and hunting season.

Behavior Parallels

You have undoubtedly observed many parallels in animal and human behavior. Mrs. Woody, Mama Squirrel and young Ben demonstrated the protective instinct. Selfishness is observed also in competition for water in the birdbath between individuals and groups. A bully dove regularly guards the bird feeder. Some deer threaten others with ears pulled back, lowered heads or walloping others with their front feet, staking a claim over what they consider their stash. We observed doe pushing away yearlings that were their precious fawns the previous season to hoard the goodies for themselves. A few share, but most act like kids who still must learn their kindergarten lesson of courtesy and sharing. Some even stomp a warning foot when they see us bringing their treats. Wariness of human beings is probably a good thing or they might become too vulnerable. Nearly all deer will intimidate an injured or disabled deer, perhaps by instinct to control damaged DNA.

Imbalance

Why do animals enact these little dramas? This universe was created perfect but is now not functioning properly (Genesis 1-3). Suffering includes all living things and the Earth itself (Romans 8:18-23). The verified second law of thermodynamics, also called *entropy*, is in place—summarized essentially that everything is winding down, decaying and *not* improving.[1, 2] DNA mutations occur, and offspring always reveals gradual degeneration with the passage of time. Mutations never reveal improvement.[3] Besides imperfect behavior and physical degeneration, out of balance

---

1. *The World Book Encyclopedia.* 1991. s.v. "Entropy."
2. Ibid. s.v. "Thermodynamics."
3. Jeffrey Thompkins, PhD. "Genetic Entropy Points to a Young Generation." 16. *Acts & Facts*, Vol. 43 no. 11; (2014). 16. Institute for Creation Research, Dallas, TX.

D. S. Spears, Ed.D.

weather brings too much prolonged rain leading to severe flooding in one area and in the same time frame sustained drought in another.

Good news resides in nature's drama—we will be rescued some day, and perhaps "soon." Biblical prophecy informs us there will be universal peace on Earth, but human beings with all their worldly philosophies cannot accomplish this:

> 6 The wolf also shall dwell with the lamb, The leopard shall lie down with the young goat, The calf and the young lion and the fatling together; And a little child shall lead them.
> 7 The cow and the bear shall graze; Their young ones shall lie down together; And the lion shall eat straw like the ox.
> 8 The nursing child shall play by the cobra's hole, And the weaned child shall put his hand in the viper's den.
> 9 They shall not hurt nor destroy in all My holy mountain, For the earth shall be full of the knowledge of the Lord As the waters cover the sea (Isaiah 11:6-9).

Only the one true God can make this happen.

Moral Of The Story
— *Practical lesson:* Take many photos of memorable events with wildlife. If you keep a journal, try drawing some.
— *Spiritual lesson:* Continue asking questions about life, and thank the Lord for all His creatures—even the creepy ones such as snakes and centipedes. There must be a reason for them beyond just balance of nature.

Little Dramas

A white wing dove on her leisurely beat,
'Round fluted petals of the birdbath rim,
Circling, and pacing before dipping feet,
Appearing uncertain of taking a swim.

Competition for goodies, a familiar scene
Acted out daily is quite amusing.
Deer hoofing, birds lifting wings looking mean,
Others undaunted continue feeding.

Masked bandits working their mischief in darkness.
Revealed in daylight by uprooted pots,
We groan and complain about this trespass,
But know the rascals think they're hotshots.

Birdbath filled with antlers touching
Of four eight-pointers drinking it dry,
Antlers raised, chin whiskers dripping,
A prize-winning photo op slipped by.

Woodpecker drains the hummingbird nectar
While alpha hummer dive-bombs his rear.
But Woody now has become a boozer,
And maintains position without fear.

Figs grow abundantly but not for us;
Birds and squirrels poke, peel or crack.
Deer leave the lower limbs leafless,
But one and all claim a good snack.

Diane Shields Spears ©

···5···

Pogo

. . . .
The rejected eventually expect rejection.
. . . .

One of six black lab puppies was a runt. The five played famously together but always squeezed the runt away from eating and from games. When weaned, their owner piled them into a cardboard box, placed them in his pickup bed and drove to the local market parking lot with a large sign that read "Beautiful Black Lab Puppies for Sale." After a long afternoon, the runt was the last pup left. The weary pickup driver waited and waited until supper time, then decided to give the runt to the next person who happened by.

James, Sylvia and their small son, Jimmy, pulled into a parking space nearby. As the family walked toward the market, the truck driver approached them with his urgent request to take the puppy because he had to leave for an emergency. He shoved the pup into the little boy's arms and hastily climbed into the pickup and drove away. The stunned family just stood there in disbelief.

James' face and voice registered astonishment. "What does that guy think he's doing? We don't want a puppy!"

"But Daddy, I'd like to keep him. He's so cute. Can we keep him? Please? Can we?"

"Well, we can't just dump him like that man did. We will look for a home for him. Honey, take Jimmy and the pup to the car. I'll get the milk and bread—and uh— what else?"

"Peanut butter and eggs, but you might as well get a bag of puppy food too."

Jimmy and Sylvia took the puppy to the car. She had to admit he was cute, although small for his breed and age. Sylvia wondered if the pup was healthy and was concerned that adding vet bills and puppy food to their budget would be quite a strain.

"Now Jimmy, don't get your hopes up. We can't keep him."

"But Mom, he needs us!"

As soon as they were in the car, the pup squirmed and wiggled out of Jimmy's arms and began jumping and climbing over them and the seats with almost alarming energy.

"Catch him!" called Sylvia excitedly. "We don't want to later find an accident in the car!" She was beginning to think of additional difficulties with a puppy besides expenses. She worked part-time and thought about the time and energy it would take to train him. James occasionally worked overtime, and Jimmy would be in kindergarten and then at Grandma's until her shift was over. It looked impossible.

Jimmy played with Pogo in the back yard until they were both worn out. Pogo rested while Jimmy had his bath. The backyard was not prepared for Pogo—the fence needed repair and nothing could be found for an outside bed. They began looking for a place in their small house for the pup that could be cleaned easily if he had an accident. They chose the bathroom and spread newspaper on the floor. It was a challenge corralling the pup since he had a resurgence of energy after his rest and was bouncing all over the house. Jimmy remarked with delight, "He looks like he's on my pogo stick!" The name stuck—Pogo.

The next morning James, still half asleep and forgetting about Pogo, entered the bathroom. The pup immediately squeezed past his legs and bounded out into the hall. James stepped barefoot in something on newspaper and began hollering. Sylvia rushed from the bedroom to investigate and Jimmy was awakened by the commotion.

"That seals it," shouted James. "He's got to go! Get that rascal right now and tie him in the back yard! We should have done that last night." Sylvia and Jimmy were silent, careful not to add to the turmoil. Sylvia rushed to clean the mess, and Jimmy chased after Pogo to tie him outside. Pogo thought it was a game, so it took quite a bit of time.

At breakfast, they discussed asking close neighbors to take Pogo, but their acquaintances in the neighborhood already had pets. Sylvia suggested, "Why don't we ask my mom if she can take him, at least temporarily until we find a permanent home."

"I suppose so. Just do something!" stated James firmly.

Jimmy teared-up but remained silent while Sylvia made the call to Grandma. He silently prayed to keep Pogo.

That afternoon, Sylvia retrieved Pogo from the back yard before picking up Jimmy at Grandma's only four blocks away. Grandma had a large old dog, Roger, that did not take kindly to the newcomer in his yard. Pogo was undaunted. Walking or running was not Pogo's style—he bounced. Grandma enjoyed watching him but thought Pogo was just too energetic for her and the older dog. Roger also growled when Pogo tried to play, then he stood guard over his food dish. Jimmy called to Pogo, but he had not yet learned his name, so he continued bouncing until he bounded in Jimmy's direction, leaping into his arms and knocking them both to the grass. Jimmy laughed, " See Mom. He likes me!"

"I'm afraid he's not going to work out here," stated Grandma rather sadly. "Do you know anyone else?"

"Not at the moment," replied Sylvia without enthusiasm. "Can you manage another day or two until we can find someone?"

"I'll ask my neighbor who lives alone with no pet now. I'll call you with the verdict."

"Can you call her now?" asked Sylvia hopefully. Grandma nodded with understanding and went to the phone.

All this time Jimmy was running and playing while Pogo was bouncing around him. Grandma returned with a smile. "Lydia said she would try!"

Jimmy reluctantly followed Grandma and Mom to Lydia's house next door with Pogo wiggling in his arms. A well-dressed woman answered the door and received the squirming pup from Jimmy's arms. "Did you name him?"

"Pogo," offered Jimmy. "But he doesn't know his name yet, so you can change it." He knew in his heart Pogo was absolutely the right name but refrained from further comment.

Lydia offered, "Won't you come in?"

"Only for a moment," replied Grandma. "This is my daughter, Sylvia, and my grandson Jimmy. We are so glad you are willing to keep him."

"He's really cute. My wonderful dog Amos died two months ago, and I miss him a lot. He was fourteen. I hope Pogo likes it here."

Lydia's living room was spectacular with beautiful vases filled with roses from both front and back yards. Sylvia had admired the roses near the front porch as they were waiting at the door. Now she was astonished at the varieties on display indoors.

"Would you like to see my garden out back?" asked Lydia. "I've been cultivating roses for many years now, and expect to produce a new variety very soon." Pogo continued wiggling, but she had a firm grip. Lydia's back yard was breathtaking, nearly filled with rose bushes and a large greenhouse. Lydia set Pogo down and he took off bouncing. They all laughed as he sprang like a gazelle. Suddenly Pogo crashed into to a bush, then another, and another. He yelped when stuck by thorns. A horrified Lydia ran to get him, but he bounded between rows away from her, continuing the damage.

Lydia began shrieking, "My roses! My roses! Get him, get him quick! Get him! He's ruining my garden!"

Pogo bounced toward Jimmy and landed in his arms knocking them into another bush. It was abundantly clear Pogo was not welcome. Lydia was sobbing loudly. Grandma and Sylvia apologized profusely, excused themselves and left quickly.

What to do? Jimmy tried to hide his relief that this might prove Pogo was truly his.

The greatly distressed pair trudged home with Pogo and

Petals Everywhere

tied him to the clothesline with a loop so he could still run but in a restricted area. Jimmy spent time petting and talking to Pogo before he retrieved his pogo stick from his room. Back outside, he bounced on the small patio while Pogo just lay on the grass and watched quietly, evidently tired from his exciting event.

Upon arriving home, James was thoroughly dismayed when he saw Pogo still in the family. Sylvia filled him in with details of the day. "Well, we can try Uncle Jack and Aunt Grace. Their dog might be young enough to play with Pogo. I'll call them after supper. We are overdue for a visit with them anyway." His determined voice matched his countenance.

The next Saturday, the family drove sixty miles to the Anderson house where they were enthusiastically greeted. "Oh, Pogo is so cute! And such a cute name!" Jimmy explained the inspiration for the name.

"Brutus needs a playmate to keep him in shape," explained Uncle Jack as they exited to the back yard. "Pogo looks energetic."

Upon spying his small visitor, Brutus, their Doberman Pincer immediately emitted a sustained and menacing bared-teeth snarl. Pogo was intimidated this time and ran behind Jimmy's legs. Uncle Jack grabbed Brutus' collar, but Brutus continued to growl, bare his teeth and strain against Uncle Jack's hold on his collar.

"Well, I don't know about this. We've never tried to get a friend for Brutus. Maybe he's jealous."

Pogo continued to cower behind Jimmy. James whisked Pogo into his arms as they retreated into the house leaving Brutus the victor. Pogo immediately had an accident on the carpet. Much hollering and grabbing Pogo quickly to remove him from the living room confused and frightened him. He was banished to the laundry room during lunch with a small bowl of milk and some of Brutus' food.

Pogo did not bounce or even wiggle in the car on their way home, nor did he bound in the back yard when tied to the clothesline.

"Daddy, something's wrong with Pogo."

"Maybe his feelings are hurt from being yelled at so much and nobody wanting him."

"But *I* want him!" Jimmy's voice cracked with emotion.

"I know, Little Man, but it's not possible."

That evening James and Sylvia decided to take Pogo to the local animal shelter for adoption. Jimmy cried himself to sleep. He declined going with Dad to the shelter after church and sat in the backyard swing barely moving his feet in the sand and hoping the shelter would be closed on Sundays. Sylvia watched him through the kitchen window while washing dishes and felt his ache.

Dad returned about an hour later with a good report—they do not destroy animals. Besides, a family was looking excitedly at Pogo when he left. Jimmy was relieved that Pogo would not be destroyed but was still not truly comforted. He stoically held back tears about his unanswered prayer. Sylvia noticed, sat with him and told him that it must not be the right timing for God to give him a dog. He understood but still was terribly unhappy. He continued to cover it.

· · · · ·

Two months passed. Jimmy still missed Pogo but had not mentioned him or even wanting a dog. He did not, however, play with his pogo stick. He had to believe a loving family had adopted Pogo, or the shelter was taking good care of him. He finally asked Dad for the name of the shelter.

"Why do you want to know? You're not still sad about Pogo, are you?" James had definitely noticed that Jimmy missed Pogo even though he had never really owned him, nor had he complained. It was obvious the boy needed a dog, so he and Sylvia made the decision they would manage somehow. He regretted having taken Pogo to the shelter, because finding an acceptable substitute might take some time.

"I want to call 'em to make sure he's OK," stated Jimmy flatly. He was unable to manage the suspense of not knowing any longer.

"Jimmy, you have to let him go." James truly believed Pogo was gone forever.

"But Daddy, I *have* to know if he's OK."

"Alright, but you might be disappointed in their answer." James made the call and the inquiry. He was silent for a couple of minutes, but then a concerned frown appeared between his eyebrows. "I'll be there with my son in just a few minutes." He hung up and hurried to to the kitchen. "Sylvia, Jimmy and I are going to the rescue shelter. I just finished talking with them and learned that a family had adopted Pogo but couldn't deal with the pup's energy and gave him to another family that was reported for abusing all their pets. Pogo's been returned to the shelter. He has some cuts and possibly a dislocated shoulder. They are x-raying him right now."

"I'm coming too." Sylvia quickly turned off the stove burner.

Jimmy had followed his dad to the kitchen and overheard all. "Daddy, he's just got to be OK! Please pray that Pogo will be OK! I don't want him to die," he sobbed.

"Jimmy, don't worry. We'll find out."

Upon arriving at the shelter, Jimmy burst through the door and shouted, "Is Pogo OK?" The assistant behind the counter told him to wait just a few minutes. Jimmy fidgeted but kept quiet. She soon reappeared and asked James to follow her. Jimmy worried. A few minutes passed before James rejoined his family and trying to hide a smile.

"Daddy, is he going to die?" Jimmy's voice shook.

"No, he's going to be healthy again," spoke an encouraging voice as the vet emerged from the back immediately behind James carrying a black bundle, somewhat larger than when Jimmy last saw him. Pogo immediately recognized Jimmy and began wagging excitedly. The vet had a firm grip. Addressing Jimmy, he explained, "Pogo's been treated badly, and he was scared when he came back to us, but he'll be OK. No broken bones, but his shoulder will be sore for several days, and he needs good food and lots of love." The vet grinned, "Can you take care of him?"

"I sure can! I won't even let him walk too much!"

"He's able to walk, but try to keep him from bouncing for a while. I remember this pup well from the first time he was here. Pogo's an excellent name. I believe he will bounce again."

On the way home, James explained to Sylvia that some of the shelter's recent grant money would be applied to Pogo's treatment and adoption fees with a payment plan for the small remainder. Any other expenses of adding him to the family would be worth it.

"You know, we still have the bag of puppy food," remarked

Sylvia softly with moist eyes. Jimmy held Pogo on his lap in the back seat grinning from ear to ear. Pogo looked like he was grinning too. Jimmy and Pogo were obviously destined for each other, and God answered his prayer.

Bouncing and Bounding Again

• •

Answered and Unanswered Prayer

Everyone who prays experiences "unanswered" prayers. Reasons vary according to the request but Scripture gives clues. First, we must ask according to God's will. Thus, knowledge of Scripture and seeking the Lord are required to know what God wants and does not want in each situation and according to His specific purpose for us. Prayers will not be answered if they are prayed "amiss" (James 4:3), that is, asking for something against what the will of God has for you personally or is against His Word.

Sometimes God brings answers quickly, but more often answers come after time in which we learn to maintain faith that God wants to bless us. Sylvia ministered to Jimmy that it must not have been God's timing to have a dog. She did not indicate that God would say "No." The whole family learned from this experience that faith in God would bring good from bad. Jimmy's answered prayer was delayed and finally confirmed without a doubt that Pogo was his. The answer came through unexpected channels. God's responses to our prayers will be "No," "Maybe," "Yes," or "Wait."

Rejection versus Acceptance

Pogo was repeatedly rejected before finding his permanent home. After repeated rejection, a person can begin to believe he or she is of little or no value. Continual rejection, if not properly dealt with emotionally and spiritually, can produce *expectation* of rejection. The understatement of the universe—not everyone is nice. We cannot expect everyone to think we are wonderful.

Every person and creature without exception is of great worth to the Lord (Luke 12:6-7, 24-31). Each of us is specially created for a specific and uniquely designed purpose. He will never reject you unless you repeatedly reject Him up to your death.

The Lord wants to be close, to be your Friend, and for you to be His friend (Proverbs 18:24). He will never leave you or forsake you (Hebrews 13:5), not even if your father and mother forsake you (Psalm 27:10). He will watch over you (Psalm 91:11; Jude 1:24; Luke 4:10). He loves you with a love so deep it will require an eternity to even begin to understand. The Lord *is* love (Ephesians 2:4; 1 John 4:7-8, 16). He loves because of Who He is, not because we deserve His love. All humans deserve the ultimate penalty of banishment from God. If we cooperate with God's directions, His grace (unmerited favor) will allow us to receive that amazing love now and for eternity.

Rose Bed

All the above about God's love is absolutely true, so what about all the troubles in life? The Lord said that everyone would have tribulation and persecution, especially Christians who are standing up for believing the Bible is God's infallible and plenary Word. Just be prepared for extra troubles in this "politically correct" world. Standing firmly for God's Word will bring heavenly rewards.

Moral Of The Story
 — *Practical lesson:* Be encouraged that rejection from people has nothing to do with your value to God.
 — *Spiritual lesson:* You do not fit in everywhere. You are specially designed to occupy a specific and unique place.

What other lessons might be contained in this parable?

Camping Stuff

••••••••••••••••••••••••••••

Altering routines can be energizing.

••••••••••••••••••••••••••••

Trips to Canada and Yosemite National Park were my limited camping experiences when I was a child, so I had no concept of the preparation required. My readiness then was to be sure Brown Bear was tucked under my arm plus my favorite books crowding the space in my suitcase.

When Truman and I planned our honeymoon, we decided to camp and ride the trails at Big Bend National Park, Texas, which has since become my favorite vacation area. We had our wedding night at his parents' lake house, so I was able to look gorgeous for him at first. Thereafter I was *au naturel*. I was already acquainted with helmet hairstyles and eating dust on primitive motorcycle trails. Many days before our wedding, we began gathering *stuff*.

Getting Ready

The preparation required for this camping trip was astonishing. Truman, an experienced camper and desert motorcycle rider, had already gathered most of the stuff in one place. My eyes watered at the spread that gobbled up about one half of his nearly triple carport floor space. We were borrowing his parents' truck bed camper, and I just could not imagine how it would all fit and was a little concerned I would have to leave something behind that I wanted to take.

The camper was not an over-the-cab or over-the-sides but quite compact with a sink and miniature cupboard on one side, and a two-burner stove, an eighteen inch closet on the other side with a portable toilet slid under it and a slide out bed at the cab end—i.e., a six-by-eight-foot space. Learning to live in a condensed space with bare necessities is a large learning experience for a new bride whose last camping experience was at age eight. I would soon learn much more than expected or thought possible in one trip.

During our engagement, Truman taught me to ride an on-off road motorcycle. It was great fun. Our motorcycles were going on our honeymoon with all the pertinent stuff. This was not going to be just an enjoy-each-other-and-the-wild-outdoors adventure. It would be a physical workout on miles of sandy, rocky trails. Besides the regular items necessary for camping: food, dishes, cooking utensils, clothes, boots, towels, extra gallons of water and . . . , we also had to stow helmets, canteens, extra gas, extra clothes, trail lunch packs and . . . It seemed overwhelming. My thought that I wisely kept to myself was, "This is so much work for one week of fun!"

The day after our wedding we returned from the lake, hooked up his motorcycle trailer behind the camper-topped truck, tightened the straps on the already loaded motorcycles, put the last minute cold items in the ice boxes, tied down an extra ice box and other boxes between the two motorcycles and out the driveway we went. That was the last of my gorgeous moments. Clues that we must have looked very unusual to others on the highway were all the turned heads from passenger windows as cars passed us. "We must look like the Beverly Hillbillies," I mused.

We have made several trips since to Big Bend with our son, Gene, who learned to ride a Suzuki JR50 with training wheels before he was three. Motorcycles in Big Bend must be street legal, so Gene could not ride his on the trails or in the camping areas until he was old enough for a license. Nevertheless, we took his then current size motorcycle on our trailer every trip, because a grand set of old mining hills in Study Butte (pronounced *Stoody Beaut*) lies just outside the NW park border where the three of us left our tire marks. Our photo albums bulge with memories of each other and scenery from our many trips to Big Bend.

We have had no single perfect or single disastrous trip. Our mini disasters and interesting incidents were spread out over several visits to Big Bend that make each trip memorable. Every major and minor experience has been part of our learning curve, especially for me.

Highlights:

1. Stopping on the main highway shoulder, I photographed impressively large deer feeding in the desert. After standing on the motorcycle foot pegs for a few miles up the mountain to the Basin (an extinct volcanic crater), I experienced pain in my legs when sitting down on the bike for the descent to the Basin. The pain was acute, and we still had a distance to ride. When we reached camp, I discovered giant red and black ants stinging my thighs. I had evidently been standing on an ant mound blithely photographing the deer and not realizing the ants had climbed the inside of my jeans. Truman prayed and all was OK.

2. Another visit required sleeping in the truck bed and front seat in the Panther Junction Ranger Station parking lot due to no vacancies. Others were there for the same reason. Big Bend is very popular, so reservations now are mandatory.

3. On another trip, Gene, then age six, and I hiked a steep path up the two-and-a-half miles to the top of Lost Mine Trail for a spectacular 360-degree view. The blacktop disappeared into rocky earth about 500 yards short of the summit. We carefully picked our way over increasingly large rocks and interesting variety of cacti on a narrow and primitive deer-like trail with hairpin windings. The final ascent is so steep in places that it required hands on the ground clutching whatever could be safely grasped—a real mountain climb.

   A surprising number of folks at the top were eating lunch, taking photos or precariously dangling their feet over a ledge! Always aware of possible consequences, I shudder to think if the outcropping gave way or they just slipped, rescue would be impossible. I am always amazed by how many people play the daredevil.

   The rough 500 yard trail was easier ascending than descending. Because Gene was too tired, I piggybacked him at least halfway down the upper rough deer trail. I slipped on the loose rocks and down we went, skinning and bruising elbows, hips, derrières and knees. We both moved rather stiffly for most of the next day

4. Harry, one of our cousins, took a desert trail curve too

rambunctiously on his motorcycle, slid into a Spanish dagger (*yucca*) and was stuck in his derrière. After the men went to the showers, Truman laughingly reported that Harry had a purple-in-the-center-tri-colored wound causing him to sit gingerly on his motorcycle for the next two days.

5. On one of our trips, Truman's mother and her two sisters accompanied us. We all decided to cross the Rio Grande River to Boquias, Mexico, a typical border tourist village. The only way to cross was with the local rowboat business at $1.00 each. We paid, climbed in with six other people besides the six of us plus the boat owner! The river was swollen from recent rains, the current was swift and the water was only three inches from the rim of the boat.

   Noticing our concerned countenances, the oarsman declared confidently, "No worry. I take mucho hombres." In the middle of the rapid current, he loudly announced, pointing his finger at the water, "My cousin, he drown here last week." Visible stiffening, eyes glancing around furtively and an audible collective sigh when we reached shore were the results of his announcement.

   We rented donkeys to carry us the one mile ascent to the village. Aunt Johnnie had the lead donkey that stopped every twenty to thirty feet to tinkle. We laughed so hard all the way to the village that we could have fallen off the donkeys, because their girth made straddling difficult.

   After drinking Cokes, strolling the one street, peering into the expected architecture of the small adobe church and purchasing small souvenirs, we walked back down to the river, hoping we would have a boat to ourselves. The donkeys' owner really seemed not to understand why we shunned riding his beloved beasts down the hill, cutting the price to $.50 per, then to $.25 cents per as he pursued us.

6. Two separate incidents of truck trouble necessitated a 150 mile motorcycle round trip for Truman to the nearest auto parts shop in Alpine.

7. Wind in the Basin blew all our food off the table more than once. We learned to clip the tablecloth corners together with

multiple clothespins, and when we were away from the campsite, to weight everything down with rocks.

8. Various clever critters raided the ice chests to party at our expense while we were out on the trails. Bananas were a special attraction. While we were sitting at a picnic table, we saw a *javelina* (wild pig species, pronounced *hav-a-lee-nah*) trying to invade our tent. Before we could shoo him away he had broken the zipper. They have sharp tusks and teeth and sometimes attack.

9. Some of the desert trails are day long trips requiring the occasional search for privacy bushes or rocks as outhouse substitutes that were not also creepy critter hide outs— always a memorable experience when one appears. We are told they are more afraid of us than we are of them. Questionable!

10. Returning to camp late one afternoon on our motorcycles, I had to hold my feet high off the foot pegs as I saw, too late, a long silver snake crossing the road. Both tires got him. At least the tires did not flip him in the air to land on me! I shudder to think of that possibility.

11. We witnessed a myriad of fascinating creatures: extra large deer, hundreds of cottontails, coyotes, javelinas, raccoons, a hummingbird as large as a canary, red and black ants as long as an adult's thumbnail, and an impressive "herd" (What is a group called?) of brown tarantulas crossing the road to the Basin motel area. Bear-proof food boxes had been installed in the campgrounds on our last two trips, but we saw no bears. We were aware of several pairs of glowing eyes in the dark at various times. Mountain lions are spotted occasionally, but we saw none.

12. We watched and listened to a nine or ten member family of javelinas snorting around our camp at night while we peered through the tent screen windows. Several came within inches of us but did not attack the tent. We considered taking photos but guessed the flash would startle them and possibly cause a stampede or an attack. Scary but thrilling.

13. Spying vultures (condors?) with wingspans extending nearly

a foot beyond each end of large picnic tables in the Basin is still shocking. Creation is amazing. (Job 38 and 39).

14. Accompanying a large group of people, we waded barefoot across a wide Rio Grande tributary in Santa Elena canyon. Sinking into thick mud under about one to eight inches of water produced suction noises with each step in the shallowest parts. Our quest was to see the endangered peregrine falcons in and around their nests precariously perched on the canyon sides. A university professor and his students were among us, and we benefited from his knowledge. Wildlife that few people are privileged to see in person is unforgettable.

15. Twice more we benefited by tagging along with university professors and their classes. We heard about the geology of the area and about the rare sighting of Haley's Comet.

16. The two-and-a-half-mile descent to and arduous ascent from the Window Trail in the Basin is worth the effort. The trail leads to a dip in the horizon between mountains where the sun sets. The trail narrows to a cave-like canyon with a lazy stream spilling its mountain-cold contents about 300 feet below to the desert floor. Innumerable photos and paintings have memorialized this location, because the sunsets beaming through the Window provide a spectacular and inspiring color break from the Basin moonscape.

Despite the few negatives, the entire Big Bend experience has been overwhelmingly worth all the preparation. We would still camp and ride in the desert if Truman and I had the energy in our later years to prepare.

Precious Lessons

1. I highly recommend camping trips for families, but an austere honeymoon camping trip has some uncomfortable and blushing moments like sharing a portable toilet space with the kitchen and bunk areas—a togetherness that breaks down all modesty attempts all at once—a get-to-know-your-spouse crash course. Nevertheless, I still would not trade it

for a colorless hotel or motel. Unlike many modern couples, we did not live together or know each other sexually before marriage. I mention this, not to be pious, but because we both respect and honor the Lord and His commandments. I suspect that decision has been a factor in our marriage lasting since 1977. Respect and trust in the marriage relationship is best established before the beginning and is priceless. This is stated also to encourage dating and engaged folks to live responsibly for successful marriages that honor the Lord. Marriage has enough challenges without adding suspicion.

2. I can do without many things this city girl deemed essential.
3. My appearance is not primary as long as I am clean, modest and not in rags.
4. We were repeatedly awed by the infinite creativity of the Creator and the grandeur of His creation. Peering through binoculars at the clear night sky from our high elevation in the Basin rewarded views of an astonishing array of stars not visible to the naked eye or where city lights interfere (Psalm 19:1-6). I had thought only telescopes could see that much.
5. Scanning miles and miles of mountains in all directions from the top of Lost Mine Trail perhaps compares with being in a glider—a little dizzying. Only birds and hushed voices of others at the summit broke the profound silence. The arduous climb was worth partaking of the panorama and serenity, even considering the stumble and fall on the way down.
6. An endless array of photo, painting and writing subjects are in nearly every turn of the road and behind every rock, tree and bush.
7. Most of our trail riding was on the numerous and challenging unpaved desert trails of gravel, half-exposed rocks, deep sand requiring paddling with our feet, deep ruts, washouts and rock slides.

One trail was the only paved trail that we knew of in that part of the park, cemented with jutting rocks for traction. Not only was it a steep (estimated fifty-dgree-plus) ascent, but also a narrow right turn around a hug rock half way up was daunting. I was unsure at first if I could negotiate it. I watched Truman ride up, disappear around the gigantic rock, and return for encouragement. Riding up for me was extremely tough, but the descent was scary. With that practice behind me, we both rode up again to continue the trail. Managing not to fall or crash always strengthens confidence.

Valuable and Essential

I believe the most precious experiences of camping are:

1. Getting away from daily distractions, routines, demands and TV/electronic devices provide clear headedness, rest for my soul and a greater sensitivity to God's presence.
2. Time seems "fuller" and more significant than when occupied with regular routines—a different realm of existence.
3. Preparing for all possible events is essential. Rarely do things succeed without preparation, and a camping trip requires a great deal of it, especially with motorcycles and equipment.

Two kinds of preparation are essential:

1. *The physical:* Preparing the stuff should be obvious. This anecdote clearly demonstrates the risk of not preparing for all possibilities that could lead to many unnecessary hardships. Stories about people who were stranded on a hot desert trail, out of drinking water and hoping for hours and hours to be rescued are part of the park's history. A few have died. We could have exhausted our supplies requiring the trip to be curtailed, not being able to treat minor injuries and many more challenges.
2. *The spiritual:* I truly believe the most important preparation for any endeavor or just plain living is prayer to maintain our Heavenly Connection. All worthwhile relationships on Earth must be constantly maintained, or they will either fail or become less important. The same care and maintenance applies to our relationship with God. He is our Source of wisdom, provision, protection and fellowship. He also will

be our Guide in every detail when we let Him. We prayed before and during each trip, so negatives were not permanent but actually had good outcomes, and we learned something from each experience.

I hope this inspires you to learn more about yourself and God, to enjoy His creation and to take a "vacation" occasionally from routines to enter into His rest.

Moral Of The Story
— *Practical lesson:* Grab the camping stuff but always be prepared for surprises.
— *Spiritual lesson:* Find the "fuller" time regularly.

What other lessons might be contained in this anecdote?

The Shed

· ·

Build your life prayerfully by following the Master Builder's Plan.

· ·

Ernest wanted to build a simple eight-by-eight-foot plywood box for a shed. "How hard can this be?" he asked self, expecting a speedy, two-day job. With no schematic to guide, he mentally calculated the amount of materials needed. Then confident he was prepared, Ernest went to the lumberyard. He then borrowed a skill saw, drill, and tape measure from his neighbor.

Ernest earnestly and enthusiastically began the next day.

1. *Day one:* Laying out the shed area with string, Ernest realized the need for a square. Finding a cardboard box, he laid it in each corner to check the angle. He raked the area within the string and leveled it as best he could. A large rock interfered with progress while trying to remove it. Giving up, he re-raked the area, added dirt and leaves to level the area with the top of the stubborn rock and raised the string to be visible over the new ground level. Already tired, he decided to quit for the day.

2. *Day two:* Ernest cheerfully framed the foundation perimeter directly on the ground and put a rock under one corner to level it, added a center brace, and began laying the floor. He discovered the length and width were not the same, the corners were not quite ninety degrees, and the edges of the flooring length did not meet the frame. Several more measurements were necessary to cut strips from a new sheet of plywood to fill the gaps. All this took so much time he decided to quit for the day.

3. *Day three:* Ernest dismissed any momentary concern about

the corners and the foundation perimeter not being quite square, reasoning that it would not affect the rest of the construction. He proceeded with framing the walls and roof, had no problems, but was too tired to continue.

4. *Day four:* Deciding the roof was next, Ernest earnestly began attaching the plywood, and learned that two four-by-eight-foot plywood panels on each side did not allow for a roof overhang. More cuts were necessary in the "canniballed" plywood panel.

5. *Day five:* Ernest remembered he needed to replace the mostly used plywood, so a trip to the lumberyard stalled any progress for the day. He bought two extra panels just in case. Still undaunted, Ernest reasoned he had earned a rest.

6. *Day six:* The walls were next, but the same miscalculation of the length and width persisted, so Ernest cut more strips from the used panel to fill in the gaps. By this time, his frustration level had risen, and he decided to postpone cutting triangles for the roof peaks until the next day. At this point, he was quite proud of his foresight for purchasing extra plywood.

7. *Day seven:* When he finished, he had a large new box with no door. He could not believe he had not planned for the door, so he grabbed the saw and began cutting an opening for the doorway using the wall edges as measurement guides. Next, he attached the cut-away section for the door with hinges (borrowed from his good neighbor) and placed it over the hole. He stood back and looked at his creation with pride. He noticed it was slightly crooked, but thought no one would notice, and it would not bother him once it was painted and bushes planted around it.

• • • • •

That night began a week of heavy rainstorms. "Oh no! Oh no! Oh nooooooooo!" Ernest exclaimed earnestly, realizing he had not thought to buy roll roofing and hoping all was OK. He was still hopeful and in expectation of painting the shed when the rain was completely gone and everything dry.

8. *Days eight to fifteen*: Day by day, Ernest watched the sad deterioration of his beloved project with mounting depression and shame. When the rain finally subsided, the pitiful shed was mud splattered, several inches out of place in the saturated ground, alarmingly tilted with two corners sunk into the mud and leaves, the door and roof had swollen and sagged and the floor buckled. Without condemnation, his neighbor graciously offered to help him tear it down and rebuild.

"Oh noooooooooooo!"

• •

Dumb and Dumber

The lack of wisdom in this ridiculously exaggerated parable is obvious, but a few comments are helpful. Some critically important steps applicable to any endeavor were ignored:

1. a specific plan outlined in detail (thinking it through),
2. a complete list of required tools, materials and equipment,
3. knowledge about creating a lasting foundation (research),
4. checking the weather forecast for an outdoor project (awareness of possible hindrances),
5. asking for help (recognition of personal limitations).

Thoughtlessness versus Instructions

Have you thrown your life together like this example? Have you ever ignored or misunderstood instructions requiring a start over?

Although full of hyperbole, the above scenario can symbolize how people sail through life without a specific plan or wisdom. Life can be cruel and does not always offer do-overs—but God does. Why do many people come to the Lord for help as a last resort? Human nature wants control, even when we know deep down that He is the only real Helper. The instruction manual for earthly and eternal life is Scripture. If instructions are not followed, results will be faulty.

The Lord Jesus taught a similar and superbly told parable in startlingly fewer words than this story (Matthew 7:26). His wise parable emphasizes Him as the solid foundation on which to build our lives by adhering to His unfailing Word. Once a firm foundation in the Lord is established, wisdom is required to build with quality materials—God's ideas and principles. It is possible to spend much time, energy and resources in building your life, and in the end not have a good structure (1 Corinthians 2:10-15) if His construction plan is ignored. He wants our lives to produce for us eternal rewards and avoid fruitless work and sweat.

The Noggin Problem

God has a specific plan for each individual (Ephesians 2:8-10). His plan is a perfect fit, but fearing His plan will impede following Him perfectly. Being honest will reveal we come short of perfection without an outside source for guidance. We make mistakes. Our noggins are finite and preprogrammed by methods and techniques of faulty, worldly brands of wisdom that promote self-improvement above all other methods, leading to "the blind leading the blind (Matthew 15:14)." The Bible is the beginning of the search that will guide you to fulfilling His tailor-made plan for your valuable life.

Moral Of The Story
— *Practical lesson:* For success, build on the Lord's foundation with quality materials (good character, wisdom and correct knowledge) using the best tools (Scripture).
— *Spiritual lesson:* Constantly measure (judge) your thoughts and actions according to God's Word to adhere to His specific plan for your life (1 Corinthians 11:31).

What other lessons might be contained in this parable?

8

Dust

If I have to dust it, I don't want it.

Many years ago I attended a meeting in the lovely home of a prosperous couple, and as the meeting progressed, the large number of knickknack displays distracted me. After the meeting, we were given a tour of the home. One very long hallway was on an outside wall with floor-to-ceiling windows and several glass shelves full of carefully arranged families of knickknacks. These curios were featured in every room on shelves and on dressers—too many for an outsider to appreciate. The question this abundance prompted was "Who does the dusting?" It looked like a full-time job for someone. The prominence of these knickknacks led me to describe the home to my mother as, "Her knickknacks have knickknacks."

Dust Catchers

The term *knickknack* is of uncertain origin (coined by a frustrated husband?). The dictionary definition [1] is "a small trivial article usually intended for ornament." The knickknack-smothered home is an example of collecting gone wild. Most of us have items that are semi-precious to us, perhaps inherited from a cherished relative or are part of a collection. Collecting is not gender-specific and can be a good investment as a business opportunity. I know a family in which the husband has gone bonkers over displaying antique tools in the home, the yard and to the point where they are hanging from the rafters in the carport. Perhaps you know someone like that?

Earthly Focus

---

1. By permission. From *Merriam-Webster's Collegiate® Dictionary, 11th Edition* ©2015 by Merriam-Webster, Inc. (www.Merriam-Webster.com).

Objects can be a source of tension. Truman complains occasionally that the house is all mine and his stuff keeps getting crowded into smaller spaces. My sweet response—he has the garage. If we are not careful, unimportant things can inflate and become the "little foxes that spoil the vine" (Song of Solomon 2:15).

The negative impression of the lovely home swallowed by knickknacks caused me to re-evaluate my décor. Have I placed too much importance on things and how my house looks? As a result, I would occasionally look at my visually rich surroundings and determine there were too many objects to dust, and I could use the dusting time for something I enjoy. My decision to eliminate dust catchers began with a few least favorite items to reduce any associated trauma. Eventually it became painless, and I began earnestly selling or donating things I had not used in a year unless they were special gifts or heirlooms. I am sure I heard my house foundation heave a sigh of relief.

Essential or Non-essential

I am not saying we should eliminate everything non-essential. I believe the Lord wants us to enjoy our stuff but not be in bondage to it, that is, hold it loosely. Scripture admonishes us to set our minds (Colossians 3:2; KJV: affections) on things above, not on earthly things. We were created for the Lord's *pleasure* (Revelation 4:11 KJV), so it behooves us to learn what that means.

What are the desirable things above? The kingdom of God appears to be focused primarily on people and events, not things. Even though God's gift to humanity of free will allows any choice, it should be obvious not every choice is beneficial. Therefore, only the Lord is to be our Master (1 Corinthians 6:12). With this in mind, consider items of vanity and pride or projects that are too time-consuming without significant personal pleasure or benefit or, more importantly, do not honor the Lord.

In order to refocus my priorities, housework is no longer at the top of the list. I keep the kitchen and bathrooms clean to save us from food poisoning or typhoid, but vacuuming and dusting happen only when they convict me. A fine line exists between caring for things that God gives or being in bondage to them. I now have fewer things to dust, and I refuse to be a slave to anything having only earthly value and no eternal value.

Dust Plus Water Recipe

Scripture states God formed humans from dust, to dust we will return and He remembers we are dust (Psalm 103:14; Genesis 2:7). All other living things on this planet also return to dust, even under water if allowed to dry. Dust is the basic material for all physical earth suits.

Science confirms dust has value as a catalyst for rain and snow clouds. Most atmospheric dust consists of powdered minerals picked up from plowing, erosion, quarries, volcanic ash and more. Some dust contains disease and fungus spores! Dust and pollen can be an uncomfortable source of allergens and air quality. Scientists report a great portion of household dust contains human skin cells and pet dander! Ugh! [2]

All earth suits are made of the basic earthly materials plus water. In other words we are mud, and if we are boiled down to let out all the steam, we are just dirt—humbling.

Higher Value

We are more than dust and water! Most sense we are eternal, except atheists who claim there is no purpose for being here and nothing after physical death. Their thinking leads ultimately to despair and unconscious fear. Honest folk realize there must be many reasons for our existence. This world is too beautiful and complex to be void of purpose. Love exists and is a powerful force, so there has to be a reason for love. What is the source?

Natural creation can be mentally and emotionally appreciated by higher thinking beings—us. Animals do not appreciate it in the same manner or extent that inspires humans beings. Is an animal able to admire a sunset? We are significantly different from other beings. We have superior communication over other creatures—a profound difference. We are able to question. There has to be some higher purpose for these unique and major differences.

---

2. *The World Book Encyclopedia,* 1991. s.v."Dust."

The Spiritual Parallel

A deeper aspect hidden in the subject of knickknacks is ridding our lives of excess baggage—useless things from a spiritual point of view. Much besides material possessions can lodge in our hearts and interfere with mental and emotional peace.

Scripture instructs us to lay aside every weight and burden that so easily ensnares or diverts us from peace (Hebrews 12:1-2). Our hearts can become overloaded with issues, such as frustration, regret, anxiety, depression, guilt and more. If not dealt with, the weight can become so heavy we cannot function. Good news! Our hearts can be cleansed of these dark, dusty knickknacks—grimy spiritual ground that our archenemy could march on.

Moral Of The Story

— *Practical lesson:* Avoid encumbering yourself with or falling under the mastery of stuff.
— *Spiritual lesson:* Check your heart for spiritual knickknacks that destroy your peace.

What other lessons might be contained in this parable-anecdote?

9

Olivia

∙∙∙∙∙∙∙∙∙∙∙∙∙∙∙∙∙∙∙∙∙∙∙∙∙∙∙∙∙∙∙∙∙∙∙∙∙∙
All life has value in unexpected ways.
∙∙∙∙∙∙∙∙∙∙∙∙∙∙∙∙∙∙∙∙∙∙∙∙∙∙∙∙∙∙∙∙∙∙∙∙∙∙

Olivia was enjoying her fame as the self-appointed beauty queen of the olive tree. Many less plump and less perfectly formed olives were jealous, disgusted with her pride and began to actually plot how to take her down. No one had any good ideas that would work, so they decided to bad mouth her and excommunicate her from all their conversations and good fun. Olivia, being so self-absorbed, was at first oblivious to their treatment, only further infuriating the group. When she realized what they were doing, she responded with accusations about how petty they were and how it only proved her superiority.

Suddenly there was a tremendous shaking. The source was a whipping stick too violent for the olives to maintain their grip.[1] All, including Olivia, lay helplessly on the tarps under the tree. Cries went up from all, but the source of the shaking paid no attention. All the olives were gathered up and sent to the press. They cried out to Olivia to see if she could help since beauty is so valued in their culture. They thought surely the source of this tribulation would pay attention to her. Olivia was overjoyed that they had exalted her again and was certain of success but was unable to gain the harvester's attention. No help came. In the press, they all began to realize they were headed for the same fate—something unknown and fearful they did not understand.

∙∙∙∙∙∙∙∙∙∙∙∙∙∙∙∙∙∙∙∙∙∙∙∙∙∙∙∙∙∙∙

---

1. An ancient method of harvesting olives. Michael Zohary. *Plants of the Bible: A Complete Handbook*. New York. Cambridge University Press. 1982. 56.

Deceiving Self

Pride is a weakness of human nature that desires recognition, is puffy and repels. It could be labeled self-worship. Olivia focused on her beauty, so highly exalted in our society. Physical beauty is and always has been worshiped, somehow equating it with superiority in all areas. Placing a higher value on outward beauty rather than inward beauty is deceptive and leads to a gradual and sneaky drift away from what is more important—good character.

Inward and Outward

Outward beauty is temporal, but inward beauty can have positive eternal consequences. What is inward beauty with no trace of pride? God loves beauty because of His creation—it is a natural outcome of His very nature. Beauty is important, although difficult to define because of its subjectivity. Scripture describes the beauty of holiness that refers to God (Psalm 29:2; 96:9)—easy to describe. He also instructs all people to be holy as He is holy (1 Peter 1:15; Ephesians 1:4; Colossians 1:21-22)—an emphasis on character. He would not require something of us if it were not possible. He is the Way to holiness and beauty (John 14:6).

The primary reason for the entire creation is to please the Lord (Revelation 4:11, KJV). Nevertheless, the world's affluent cultures seem to be majoring in selfish pleasure, entertainment, outward show, status and possessions. All this displaces holiness in our hearts unless we have a solid connection to the Lord.

Short-sighted

The olives were destined to be a blessing to many, but they were ignorant of the reason for their existence and were unable to rejoice. Losing sight of purpose can happen when societal pressures and negative circumstances surround. Ignorance of our purpose will cause us to wander through life without true contentment or vision.

Contentment is not identical to happiness, nor is it settling for undesirable situations. Contentment is more related to joy and contains the peace and reassurance that all circumstances are temporal, and we have a Heavenly Helper who will work things out for our good (Romans 8:26-30)—if we give Him permission.

Happiness Versus Joy

The difference between happiness and joy is profound. Happiness is temporary and is based on circumstances of the moment. It is an emotional response of the soul (mind, will, and emotions) plus the physical body (endorphins) to an outside source. Happiness vanishes when the "olive press" of life begins its squeeze and negative emotions take over.

Joy and contentment are deeper, are spiritual principles and are not affected permanently by negative circumstances. True joy will sustain us through difficulties so that surrendering is not an option. Peace reigns in the midst of confusion and bewilderment when trusting the Lord has been *practiced*.

God's Word addresses all life issues, assures us of His purpose for each individual and directs the U-turn from defeat by confirming His infinite *agape* love for us. Eventually all will be turned around for good when everything is submitted to Him. Reminder: He never barges in without an invitation.

God's Symphony—You

True joy does not exist apart from God. Therefore, self-effort cannot manufacture joy—it will be a counterfeit. We need His joy because *it is His:* "Do not sorrow, for the joy *of the Lord* is your strength (Nehemiah 8:10b, emphasis added)." If our spirits are not connected to God's life, all the soul's talents and abilities will not bring joy or produce good fruit for eternity, causing us to miss our ultimate purpose and rewards (Ephesians 2:10). God wants to create a beautiful symphony of our lives.

Moral Of The Story

— *Practical lesson:* Outward beauty, status and possessions are temporal. Inward beauty is eternal and comes from the Lord.
— *Spiritual lesson:* God will use the "olive press" of life, when submitted to Him, to mold your life into a beautiful full orchestra symphony.

What other lessons might be contained in this parable?

Blacks and Whites

Percussion in my heart produces the pace
For my personal and unique melody.
My soul and my ears reject or embrace
Monotony of hovering around middle C.
The full range of notes on the blacks and whites
Still restrict my need to express
The angst of depths, breadths and heights—
Contradictions, tensions, melancholy and zest.
The tune on the keyboard only starts
To address the complex and diverse parts.

Strings in my heart catch my attention
To sliding pitches of in-between notes.
Forte and pianissimo leave an impression
Of challenging cliffs and slippery slopes.
Composition becomes increasingly complex
By adding staccato and pause.
Rehearsing what's written only reflects
The need to correct harmonic flaws.
Current sound waves—still incomplete;
It isn't enough to simply repeat.

Crucial are soothing wind instruments,
Infusion of breath to woo and caress,
Integrating all existing components,
Adding touches of expertise and finesse.
A composition theme now stitched and woven:
A purpose heard and understood with the soul,
Inspired by the Lord's will and chosen
To guide me to His highest goal.
White parchment and black notes record
My personal symphony composed by the Lord.

Diane Shields Spears ©

10

Unlikely Friends

••••••••••••••••••••••••••••••••••

Self can sabotage self.

••••••••••••••••••••••••••••••••••

A young tangerine cat named Dude lived with a kind woman who took employment in a foreign country and sadly, could not take him with her. All animal shelters were full, no neighbors or acquaintances were willing to adopt Dude, and she ran out of time before she had to leave. She had heard that cats are territorial, and will adopt whoever lives at the cat's address, so she consoled herself with the thought that a new family in the house would adopt such a beautiful cat.

Dude was left behind with a large full food dish and water on the back porch. She had spoken softly to him before she left while petting him and crying, but, of course, he only knew she was showering love on him. He had never learned her spoken language, but recognized his name and understood her love completely. He was puzzled about her absence and hung around for a few days.

Dude was accustomed to being pampered, so he was unskilled at hunting. Although the back yard had a birdbath and feeder with plenty of visitors, he had not been successful. He never understood why, because he was unable to hear himself move even a blade of grass when stalking.

When his food bowl was empty, he eventually wandered to a large ranch watering hole for livestock. From his hiding place under a bush, he watched cattle, goats, birds and dozens of other animals come regularly for a drink. During the night, he observed deer, raccoons, opossums and one juvenile mountain lion, all of which outweighed him and made him nervous. He had found only a leftover from another predator, a partial road kill and crumbs in a dog food bowl during his wanderings, so he was hungry. Dude crept from under a bush and crouched on the watering hole bank. He marveled to himself, "This is the biggest birdbath I've ever seen! Fabulous! Look at the choices! I should find a place to live around here!"

His first attempt at a capture was a frisky squirrel that escaped up the nearest tree trunk. In the chase, all birds took flight and other wildlife scattered simultaneously, actually startling Dude. "There must be an easier way," he mused. He needed a mentor.

At dusk on Dude's second day at the watering hole, the young mountain lion spied Dude, approached him stealthily and was confident he could grab him. Always on alert, Dude alluded him, circled around behind and followed closely. Suddenly, the mountain lion stopped. His long tail unexpectedly swatted Dude's nose, prompting Dude to bite the tail by reflex action. The mountain lion jumped high and wheeled around thinking it was a snake, causing Dude to freeze. He was astonished when he saw Dude behind him.

"Are you the snake that bit me?" he questioned roughly.

Dude's voice shook, "I'm not a snake! You hit me with your tail. I didn't mean to bite you, but I thought you were hunting me to eat me!"

"That was my intention! In fact, I might still do it!" threatened the mountain lion, eyeing Dude menacingly.

Dude Steeled Himself to Look Fierce.

"Well, go ahead, just try it! You don't know what you're getting into!" Dude steeled himself to look fearsome as he reared up on hind legs, sparred and hissed.

The surprised mountain lion stood motionless, staring at Dude. "Are you a cat?"

"Yes, of course I'm a cat!" replied Dude indignantly. "You're just a big overgrown kitty yourself!"

"Hey now, cut the insults. I could still eat you if I wanted to, but your kind is not as tasty as the other choices around here. I'm sorry I called you a snake. I can see now that you're a miniature me. How did you get to this ranch?"

Dude's voice changed to sad as he related the abandonment by his owner. "I don't know what happened. I hung around for a while but then decided I'd better find something to eat and ended up here."

"You mean someone *owned* you? I've heard about being a pet. What was it like?"

"She fed me every day, stroked my fur and let me snuggle with her at night. I sure miss her. The problem now is how to get my own food. I've tried hard but can't seem to get the knack of it. I'm pretty hungry right now. I found a sleeping lizard yesterday but nothing today. The birds seem to see me coming. I can creep so quietly I can't hear it myself, but I never caught anything even when I lived with my owner. They always seemed to know I was there. I just don't get it." Dude began to feel even more depressed.

"My name's Mighty Hunter," stated the mountain lion proudly. "What's yours?"

"Dude. Did you earn your name by being ferocious or did your mama name you?"

"I asked you your name," repeated Mighty Hunter with narrowed eyelids and sounding a bit peeved.

"I told you, Dude. My name is Dude."

"Oh, I see. I thought you were calling me dude trying to be cool. Dude is an odd name for a cat but I like it. Kind-a describes all us felines as superior individuals. My mama was killed when I was very young. She called me something, but I don't remember. I've had to fend for myself, so I chose that name to remind me to be courageous," he admitted. "Hey, let's be friends. I've never had a friend before, and I kind-a like your spunk."

"Yeah!" exclaimed Dude. "I've never had a friend either except for my owner. Let me know if you ever decide I'm tasty. Can I just call you 'Mighty'?"

"Sure. Why don't you let me teach you how to hunt? I'm getting pretty good at it now, and I can give you some pointers."

"I'll take you up on that. Can you do it now? I'm really hungry, and getting weak," complained Dude dramatically trying to work on any sympathy Mighty might have.

"OK, let me see you in action."

Mighty Hunter observed from a short distance. Crouching low while stealthily crossing the grass to the water's edge, Dude crept to pouncing distance on a mouse. Again, it was a failed attempt as the mouse leaped in the air and sped away. He continued, startling a lizard beyond pouncing distance while grabbing a cricket, but all the field mice seemed to be aware of him. He crept back to Mighty Hunter, complaining and dejected that the first mouse must have notified all his relatives.

Hunting by Moonlight

"Du-u-ude," spoke Mighty with an instructive tone. "You're waving your tail while you're getting ready to pounce! You might as well be waving a *Here I Am* flag!"

"I'm not waving my tail!" protested Dude at high pitch in

disbelief. "I'm *perfectly* still!"

"No, Dude, you *are* waving your tail! All us cats deal with this internal conflict. Your excitement and anticipation are sabotaging your goal. All it accomplishes is that your dinner sees you. I've had to learn this too. You asked me to help you, and I'm trying! You know, friends tell each other the truth, don't they? Well, I'm telling you the truth! *I am!*" Mighty Hunter sounded offended. Dude quickly and profusely apologized.

Dawn was breaking, ducks landed on the water and other wildlife reappeared while the ranch cattle and goats pushed their way through. Mighty Hunter suggested he and Dude sneak to the other side where possible breakfast would be unaware of them. "Wait here and watch," whispered Mighty proceeding to stalk. He crept so close to a mallard that the unfortunate duck should have felt his breath. Mighty pounced with amazing speed and stealth for his size—almost a blur. He returned proudly with the mallard dangling from his mouth.

"That was grrrrrreat!" gushed Dude loudly, instantly alerting and scattering all wildlife and ranch stock, leaving the watering hole to an unconcerned bull.

"Now, look what you've done," chided Mighty. "They might not come back before we get hungry again. I can sure see that your excitement and enthusiasm, as wonderful as they are, really work against you."

He continued instruction and advice while sharing the mallard with Dude. "Now that you know the cause of your difficulties, you should be able to concentrate on every body part being perfectly still. We'll practice more tonight on mice and at dawn on more ducks. Come with me now so I can show you where I live. We need to rest, and I have plenty of room. You are welcome if you haven't already picked a spot."

"Hey, thanks. I do want to see where you live. These nights have been chilly." Dude followed Mighty to his den and was impressed. "Yeah, I like your hole. I hope I can stay a long time."

"Sure, as long as we get along, which looks good. I do reserve the right to evict though."

Mighty Hunter helped Dude perfect his hunting skills so they were both able to bring food to the den. Dude found a wife on the ranch and invited her to Mighty's den. Mighty Hunter was mightily disturbed about not being asked first, but then realized when kittens came, he would be an uncle and he beamed visibly. Mighty fell in love too and fathered cubs. Both Dude and Mighty became uncles and grandpas several times over and eventually had to find separate living quarters, but they remained buddies all their lives.

• •

Kinds of Friends
A friendship between a young mountain lion and a cat, feral or domestic, is highly unlikely, because mountain lions will eat most anything if hungry enough. The subject of unlikely friends should spur thinking about our friendships. On analysis, most friendships are based on common interests or just enjoying the fellowship. Those are "likely" friends.

Mighty Hunter made an important statement that true friends tell the truth to be helpful, even if at first it hurts or is not believed or received. Sometimes friends are hesitant to give advice for fear of offending. However, a true friend like Mighty was not afraid to offend Dude with truth. It takes courage and love to deliver truth.

Re-learning for Success
Have you ever been told you are sabotaging your own effort—you are your own worst enemy? Other people tend to see our flaws or problems before we do. Getting advice from teachers, coaches and other non-biased professionals is wise. All need advice occasionally from those taught by experts who have discovered strategies that work best, done the hard work of practicing and can demonstrate how to correct difficulties.

Finding the Best Source
Who is the best teacher to prepare us for eternity? What is the very best source of information? Major religions all have their own bits and pieces of truth, sets of personal guides, teachers, manuals and writings. Which one is best? First, look at the fruit. Is the doctrine

about love or hate, help or destruction, fear or faith, life or death? Always look deeper than the adherents of any particular religion, because significant variations and interpretations of the precepts and doctrines exist within groups. Judging any belief system solely on people who cling to it is unfair, because some do not know or understand all of the group's beliefs. When researched thoroughly, you will discover Christianity *properly understood* is the one faith system that deals successfully with the major problem at our core— the root of self-exaltation—that stinky pride.

Likely and Unlikely

Think about a friendship between God and human beings. Does it seem unlikely? This "Unlikely Friend" is the Lord Jesus, the Christ, the Messiah. He was not afraid to tell the truth even when it hurt or angered his enemies. He is the best teacher because He has already endured the hard work of living righteously and can instruct us for success. The true story about this Unlikely Friend can be found if you allow yourself the time to search Scripture. Many concepts will come together that have not made any sense to you in the past. If you are sincere to the bone about finding truth, you will find it.

What dynamics existed in this story between Dude and Mighty, these two unlikely friends? First, Dude was initially afraid of Mighty's motives. Fear eventually turned into trust and respect that was never again questioned. Second, Mighty was sincerely willing to help without hurting him. The same happens in our relationship with God. First, we may fear His motives. "What does He want me to do?" "Is He going to punish me?" "Will He make me go to Africa as a missionary?" God never forces anyone to do anything. He has given us free will.

Spending time with the Lord and getting to know the truth about Him brings the realization that He intends only good and blessings. He is for us, is never against us (Romans 8:35-39), and His will is a perfect fit for our interests and abilities. He can become our Best Friend, if we give Him permission.

Our Unlikely Friend became like one of us, was obedient to His purpose of being our substitute in death, taking upon Himself the punishment we deserve and bringing us back into fellowship with the Triune God (Philippians 2:8). He will be our Ultimate Friend if we let Him.

Moral Of The Story

— *Practical lesson:* True friendships, like marriage, must be regularly maintained with love and time.
— *Spiritual lesson:* Get to know our Ultimate Friend, the Lord Jesus Christ, the Messiah, more every day.

What other lessons might be contained in this parable?

Dare To Dream

• •
God has the best ideas.
• •

Have you ever had a dream, vision, daydream or goal that seemed too far-fetched to come true? Even the phrases *far-fetched* and *come true* place dreams in the precarious mental category of fantasy or never-never-land.

Dreams are classified as visions of the night, visions of the day (daydreams/aspirations) and simply goals motivated by hope and interests. Whatever the category, dreams are workings of the soul (the ingredients of human personalities) and sometimes of the human spirit.

Sleep dreams can be silly, entertaining, puzzling, clothed with universal or personal symbolism that challenge interpretation, help resolve internal issues, bring solutions to problems, be frightening or prophetic. Eyes-open daydreams and visions can be just wishful thinking or be charged with strong desire.

Everyone should have at least one dream of seeing, becoming or experiencing something not yet realized—a life goal. As goals are met, seeking the Lord for new ones will avoid a decline in how we value our lives. God's work continues—He never leaves us to stagnate, but we could choose that simply by not cooperating with Him.

How do we know if night dreams are "pizza" dreams, creative reconstruction of inner information already known, something that sheds light on a problem or are from the Lord? Is it an unrealistic hope-and-ambition dream beyond achieving? Confiding in a friend can be beneficial, but the Person you can trust with the best advice is the Lord, who wants to be our Best and Ultimate Friend.

We might not know if our dream is achievable unless we *set out*—not just try—to achieve it. The word *try* infers possible defeat. Thomas Edison is known to have failed a monstrous number of times before achieving success in inventing the light bulb but did not give up. Amazing persistence and positive attitude!

Challenges

Everyone has lack of expertise in one or more areas—physical, emotional and intellectual. Some deficiencies are obvious and some hidden, even from consciousness. The majority of us will never be Hollywood handsome, Barbie beautiful or Einstein smart, and even the verified geniuses are deficient in some area. Trauma, physical appearance, poor education, lack of support and more can disable a dream. Whatever abilities or lack thereof, manifested or latent, everyone can dream to accomplish something meaningful and then pursue it to fruition. Each person has value in the Lord and needs a dream. The best dreams come from Him.

Making It Real

Ambition and goal dreams must be tried in the fire of sometimes intense and excruciatingly hard work with patience and a willingness to "pay the price." Bringing a goal dream into reality from fantasy or "unreachable-ness" requires some practical and specific steps:

1. Write the dream/vision (Habakkuk 2:2-3) in detail for mental clarity. Memory can fail with details.
2. Submit it to the Lord and write the steps He reveals.
3. Wait for His go-ahead at each step! Patience will temper hyper-excitement that can cause missteps.
4. Prepare for hard work, not just with personal effort but also in obedience to the Holy Spirit's leading.
5. Expect opposition from our archenemy who wants us to fail. Apply the wisdom of Scripture that has the power to work on your behalf—the only effective weapon to defeat the enemy.
6. The major part of defining a dream goal from the Lord is the time spent in prayer and studying Scripture.

Goal dreams can seem unrealistic or impractical. Be careful not to sabotage a good idea from the Lord by feelings of inadequacy or disbelief. God will enable you to accomplish anything if it is from

Him. Act in faith as God directs. What kind of faith? Faith in self is a cracked foundation and a dead end. True faith is not blind but focuses on the Lord. He gave us brains and minds, but since we are finite, we need guidance. The Lord says to ask Him for wisdom in every situation and He will not scold us (James 1:4-6). He knows a heap more than we do and is willing to meet that need for assistance in this complex world.

Your Purpose

The Lord's tailor-made plan for each person demonstrates how valuable we are to Him (Jeremiah 29:11; Ephesians 4:8). This specific purpose will cause us to excel, and we will love it—He has success in mind for us. He places talents and interests in us when we are created. He wants us to know what to do with them.

Goal dreams usually relate to traits, talents or interests you have already, but keep your heart open to the Lord Who can stimulate with something new. He always gives what is needed to fulfill His plan. We sometimes impatiently struggle with God's timing wanting answers and immediate fulfillment. Patience allows a growing process to hone the dream to "manageableness," and we mature spiritually in the process.

Uncertainty of purpose can cause many detours. A university classmate changed his major five times if remembered correctly. I hope he has found his niche. Most of us have several functions such as concurrent earthly roles in families and communities. The Lord's designs for us may not be earthshaking, but every person is of great worth to Him, and fulfilling His plan will shake your earth for good results. All steps are significant. You will find peace, hope and fulfillment even if your life position is deemed insignificant. In this current culture, being a homemaker is often relegated to lower class citizenship. Sometimes women, when asked what they do, respond with, "I'm just a housewife." How sad. Our nation desperately needs homemakers to raise mentally stable and healthy children. Pursue your goal if you are certain it is from the Lord.

Something Greater

An over-arching purpose—a grand spiritual purpose (in addition to personal, earthly goals) is the fact that God the Father wants us to be like His Son (Romans 8:29-30). Character development will be more fully addressed in later chapters and in the sequel to come. Nothing is impossible with God—in fact, all things are possible with Him, even the challenges that seem too great or impossible (Matthew 19:26; Mark 9:23).

Dare to dream!

Moral Of The Story

— *Practical lesson:* Give yourself permission to dream big, day and night.
— *Spiritual lesson:* Discuss your goals and ambitions with the Lord, asking for direction.

What other lessons might be contained in this devotional?

Dream

A sleeper in a semi-dream—
A dreamer in reality.
Hopefulness casts a precious beam
Of light in shade and uncertainty.
Today my dream is in the light
Of wakefulness and activity,
Then clothed with mystery of night
To be rewoven in identity.

A dream unchanged in pattern and form
In sunlight finds consistency,
And in shadow can be reborn
With insight and originality.
But shadow dreams aren't easily read,
And vanish in obscurity.
Can dreams of day and night be wed
In daylight plans and possibilities?

If I tune my intuition,
Would I find with surety
A pattern of reconciliation
With seeming diversity?
Comparing dream states compels me
To guess what circumstances mean;
As wakefulness in a large degree
Hold patterns of the deeper dream.

Diane Shields Spears ©

Mack's Journey

Everyone's journey requires signposts of faith.

Mack McRoo, the only descendant of Argus and Eeleen McRoo, two kangaroo missionaries from Down Under, lived meagerly in the Bush and daily found their own food. Argus taught Mack how to kick-box, and he became quite good at it. When Mack was very young, he was orphaned by a crocodile attack while crossing a river with his parents to establish a new ministry. Mack's parents fought and kicked, but Argus was drowned and eaten. Eeleen managed to get Mack to shore but died with severe injuries. Mack stayed with her trying to get her to speak until buzzards arrived and he had to flee. Their belongings landed on the river bottom leaving him destitute. He cried for hours. He called out to God and received some comfort but no answer yet.

Mack knew he needed to do something but had no clues. He continued questioning, "Why—Why—Why?" No answer came. Confused and afraid he had somehow been responsible, he urgently asked God to forgive him just in case. Besides, he was afraid to be alone. He began wandering, looking for someone to tell about the attack. The first being he met was a field mouse and introduced himself with a simple, "Hi."

"Who are you?' queried the suspicious mouse, eyeing Mack's huge feet and posturing as if ready to run.

"Don't be afraid. I won't hurt you. I just want to ask a question. See, my parents were killed and I want to know why."

"I can't help you. I don't know nuttin," was the mouse's cold response. "But watch out for snakes, lions, dingoes and a large critter with a loud stick and a net." Mack's parents had already warned him about those creatures. Dejected, Mack thanked the mouse and traveled on with heavy steps.

"Dear God," he earnestly prayed. "I really want to know why and what to do."

The next creature he met was a creepy one. As Mack moved through tall dry grass looking for better pickings, he noticed silent movement of grass blades. A huge snake popped up its head without warning, stared menacingly and hissed, "Thissssss issss my grasssss, ssssso get lossssssst—now!"

"I'm already lost!" shouted Mack in frustration and with the temptation to kick-box, then remembered some advice from his dad: "You don't need to start a fight but don't run from one." He could hear his dad's voice in his head that brought tears to his eyes. He was unsure which situation applied now.

"Oh, sssssssilly crybaby!" taunted the scary snake. "Sssssscram now or I'll…"

"OK, OK. Don't get your knickers in a twist!" Mack was unsure what that meant, but his parents had said it and it seemed fitting now. As he carefully backed away, he caught sight of the

"Don't get your knickers in a twist!"

retreating snake and realized it was not venomous. He had let the snake deceive him. He justified his fear by convincing himself the snake was probably one of those that squeeze until your eyes and guts pop out. He and his young friends at his old home had discussed those. Very scary.

Mack moved on looking for good grass and leaves, but sparse rain that season had left the vegetation mostly dry and tasteless. He was hoping to find a kangaroo mob to join. He kept wandering and wondering what to do. The question "Why?" never ceased to play in his young head and heart.

Spying a pride of lions in the distance, he made a sharp turn around them, eventually traveling to a wooded area. Sitting to rest in the umbrella-like shade of a huge tree, a colony of rabbits began encircling him. He was astonished at the size of this furry crowd, all wiggling their noses and uttering little nasal squeaks. One boldly approached Mack with a formal, "How do you do?"

"How do you do yourself," responded Mack, too tired to be civil. Then realizing he must have sounded sour, added, "Sorry. I'm bushed. Gotta rest—maybe sleep."

"I seeeeeeeeee," responded the rabbit studying Mack intensely. "Say, before you go to sleep, do you want some fresh grass?"

Mack perked up, "Sure! Thanks."

Two rabbits began pushing clumps of grass with their noses toward Mack, who hungrily grabbed them, began gobbling and with stuffed mouth managed to ask, "Do you have more?" His mother had always said Mack had a healthy appetite.

"Not right now. We are very late for a very important meeting to learn better protection strategies."

"Hey, before you go, can I ask you something?"

"Yes, but be quick. We're in a hurry and don't want to be any later for this very, very important date."

Mack related his tragic event, including every disappointing encounter and ended with the persistent "Why?"

The rabbit responded sadly, "We'd like to know that too. Lots of us keep disappearing, so that's why we're in a hurry. Sorry." They left as quickly as they had arrived.

Mack took a lengthy nap and was exceedingly hungry when he

awoke. He nibbled some unfamiliar leaves and grass that introduced new tastes and hoped they were healthy. He rested again digesting for a while, still asking God "Why?" Not waiting for God to answer, he decided to continue his journey.

The countryside began changing to rolling hills with plenty of green, moist grass. He grazed while walking, not looking up and was suddenly in the middle of several dozen sheep. They sounded a "baaaaaaa" chorus and scurried nervously around him. One larger ram stood in front of Mack as if to block him. Mack mustered all the courage he could and greeted the ram with his simple, "Hi!"

"Hi, yourself!" stated the ram flatly. "What are you doing in the middle of my ewes? You're not a sheep."

"I know that!" Mack relaxed slightly. "I've been looking for an answer to a very important question. Actually, it's a big question everyone might want the answer to."

"Well, we're just dumb sheep, or that's what we hear from some creatures who carry big loud sticks. We don't know much. We have someone who takes care of us and carries a stick but it doesn't make any noise. He probably has an answer. The only problem is that we don't know how to talk to him. He talks to us, and his voice and whistle sound real good to us so we follow him. He also takes us to good grass. I don't know how to ask him your question. What's your question anyway?"

Mack proceeded to relate the sad events and ended with the ubiquitous "Why?"

"I'll bet our stick man knows but like I said, we don't speak like he does. I'd like to know the answer to that question too. We've had some hardships lately. Just a couple of days ago a dingo got one of our lambs. We cried and cried and our stick man found the dingo and killed him, but the damage was done."

"Can I go meet your stick man who takes care of you? Maybe he would take care of me too. I am not grown up yet, you know."

"I dunno. He's really good to us, but I know he doesn't want any outsiders with us."

"But I wouldn't be any trouble," protested Mack. "In fact, I might be able to fight off a dingo. I could help. I can kick-box really good." Hopefulness rang in Mack's voice.

They all chorused, "What's kick-box?"
"Let me show you." Mack proceeded to demonstrate.

"Let me demonstrate."

Suddenly the stick man appeared and thinking the flock was in danger, began flailing his staff in the air and shouting at Mack. He scared Mack so thoroughly that he ran nearly a mile before stopping. Out of breath, he sat down and cried. Here was another thwarted chance to learn the answer and to have a family again. He knew he did not dare return to show the stick man he could help them. After a few minutes in which he decided he must get tougher, he began his wandering again, this time making a wide berth around other flocks of sheep and their stick men.

Mack had grown tired from traveling for miles with few rest periods and sat down under a tree, when he suddenly heard a voice above him speak softly. "I'll bet you're hungry." Mack looked up to see a koala peering down at him. "Here, have some leaves." The koala dropped several freshly plucked leaves from her perch.

"Thanks. I mean, really thanks! There's not much good grass growing here, the bushes are withered and tough, and the trees are too tall for me to reach the leaves. I really needed this."

"You're welcome. My name's Clementine. What's yours?"

"Mack McRoo."

"Where are you going?"

"Don't know. A crocodile killed my parents just a few days ago while we were crossing a river to a mission field. I don't know what to do. I've been walking around trying to get an answer to why God let it happen. I *must* understand why."

Cousins

"I'm not the one to ask, but I do know someone who can help. By the way, do you know we're cousins?"

"We don't look alike."

"And that's good. I don't think I could manage big feet or a tail like yours. However, I do think you're cute and we can be friends. I can cut leaves for you, and you can help protect me."

"You said you know someone who can help me?" asked Mack with a voice full of hope.

"Yes, his name is York and he's a Roo like you only grown up. He and his wife Heddy travel to these parts regularly, so if you want to wait for them, I can help you build a shelter."

"Sounds good. Can you drop some more leaves on me now? I'm still really, really, *really* hungry."

"OK! OK! Got it!"

After Mack stuffed his face, he grew sleepy. Sweet Clementine watched over him like a true friend until he awoke.

• • • • •

Several weeks passed before York and Heddy came. In the interim, Clementine and Mack became great friends and played famously together. She told Mack more about York and Heddy who were missionaries like his parents, so Mack immediately bonded upon meeting. They began teaching him more about God, loving and caring for him as a son. Mack grew in understanding of the "whys" and "what-for's" of bad things happening to good creatures. He learned about the great difference between good and evil, who the sources of each are and that God did not kill his parents. He decided that everyone desperately needed this information. He was beginning to understand his purpose in life.

• •

Critical Difference
A vast difference exists between good and evil. Simple theology: God is 100 percent good and Satan is 100 percent evil. This makes accurate discernment about people and events easier.

Blame and Judgment
God is blamed for many things. Many natural disasters are part of the fallen condition of this world plus human tampering with nature and poor development planning. Considering all catastrophic weather events, tornadoes seem to be the most "evil" and are the

most unpredictable. Tornado "unexplainables," such as a bathroom tissue roll embedded in a tree trunk and a grocery store leveled leaving one long shelf standing with groceries still in place, make us scratch our heads in astonishment.

Satan, not God, is responsible for some destruction while tempting us to question God's goodness, aiming to disable our faith. However, when God judges with a natural event, His judgment is for correction because of His infinite and unfailing love and His desire to commune with us as friends. Human beings should take the hint, receive the correction and change direction. The Lord is ultimately in control of the universe, but leaves many decisions to faulty humanity who messes with the environment. Therefore, when natural disasters spread destruction, we should be asking, "Who is responsible—humanity, the Devil, or God?

"Attention-Getters"

Old Testament Scripture reveals the pattern for how the Lord works with *nations* for repentance. The Israelites constantly strayed from God's presence and ordinances. He sent prophets for hundreds of years with warnings while using natural events to awaken them. They understood the cause, would repent, and God repeatedly demonstrated His mercy by delaying judgment, giving them more time to be sincere. Sin and repentance became a repeated cycle stretching the Lord's patience, grace and mercy. However, like a failed vaccination against disobedience, they rebelled against Him until their hearts were unresponsive. God sent a variety of disasters to get their attention that increased in intensity and frequency beyond attention-getters to judgments. Does this make you think about current worldwide events?

The same ubiquitous question "Why?" is asked by all when natural disasters manifest. When a nation's morality and laws degrade to the point of grossly violating God's laws, God will reveal the remedy, but not everyone is listening or will acknowledge it. That answer is whole-scale repentance from neglecting, disobeying and rejecting God to returning and worshiping Him as supreme King of the universe. God is the same yesterday, today, and forever (Hebrews 13:8). This means his correction methods in the past are strong clues to future discipline. God has not and will not change His methods of dealing with humanity's rebellions.

True Love

God is absolute, pure love (1 John 4:8, 16; Ephesians 2:4) and so much more. He is holy (1 Samuel 2:2; Psalm 99:5, 9). He is just (Isaiah 45:21; Psalm 7:11) and He is a Father in every sense. Think about what it takes to be a good parent—one who loves and corrects from that love. A good parent disciplines and guides from love so we will eventually learn self-discipline to fulfill our purposes. If the grown-ups do not correct children under their authority, the kids pick up the signal the adults do not care about them or what kind of trouble the children might cause. Uncorrected children will not believe they are loved by anyone.

The perception of not being loved is subconsciously applied to God the Father, making it difficult to have a relationship with Him. Young children want guidance and correction. They may kick, scream and fume but with determination, respect and obedience will manifest. Correction is the other side of the "love door." God's perfect love opens the door of our hearts to know Him and the value of correction that will keep us close to Him.

The nature of God's holiness requires justice—judgment and condemnation of evil—to eradicate evil from us because He wants every person to be with Him. None can come into God's presence without first repenting and submitting to cleansing or they will not survive the fire of His presence. He does not want anyone destroyed, so He protects us from His presence if we have not allowed Him to first cleanse us, even though He yearns for close fellowship with us.

God the Father has a specific route to take for cleansing. The way is repentance with the born again experience of receiving the Lord Jesus Christ, the Messiah, as Savior and Lord.

The Right Kind of Fear

A critical lack of the "fear of the Lord" in this age is noticeable. *Respect* for God's Person (His nature and abilities) is part of the fear of the Lord. "And do not fear those who kill the body but cannot kill the soul. But rather fear Him who is able to destroy both soul and body in hell (Matthew 10:28." We should also be humble and even tremble if we forget that God will discipline us if we do not discipline ourselves.

Causes for Tragedies

The world is full of trouble and heartache, but not all are a result of our poor choices or from God as punishment or correction. Mack was not responsible for his tragedy, and it was not discipline from God. This world is ailing from Adam's fall that allowed Satan to do his dirty deeds. Events caused by other people or creatures may happen through no fault of the victim. In addition, self-examination is always wise to see if better decisions could be made.

Keep On Truckin'

Hope is coming. God has promised to restore the Earth like new, evil will be permanently judged and God's love will prevail. Until then, troublesome events will be unexplainable any other way than by attributing them to either humanity's mistakes, God's judgment or the dirty deeds of the "prince of the power of the air"—Satan (Ephesians 2:2)—who is still determined to destroy us and God's plan for this globe. He refuses to give up and neither should we.

Moral Of The Story

— *Practical lesson:* We win when we stay *in* Jesus Christ, the Messiah. *In* Him is the safest place.
— *Spiritual lesson:* Learn what it really means to be in Him. (Gospel of John chapter fifteen)

What other lessons might be contained in this parable?

1,000 Pieces

A thousand piece puzzle tumbled,
Scattered, scrambled, making no sense,
Challenge to progress, confidence humbled,
Missing box cover a hindrance—
No photo of the whole for a guide,
With few clues for reconstruction.
All hope nearly died
In resisting frustration.
Can scattered pieces overturned
Be transformed to lessons learned?

Finding borders is a start,
Turning pieces for serious scrutiny
Of groups that make no sense apart,
As if participants in mutiny.
Are pieces missing? Are all present,
Are some damaged beyond repair?
Surely every piece is meant
To be included without error.
Edges found and set in order,
Bring hopefulness with the border.

A thousand pieces placed correctly,
Fitting effortlessly without forcing,
What seemed like chaos now perfectly
Unites the image endorsing
Illumination, wholeness and restoration.
Regardless the reason for the mix
Or cause of temporary halt in vision,
God's help and time are needed to fix
The whole picture to clear the mystery,
Making sense of what's now history.

Diane Shields Spears ©

13

A Thousand Pieces

••••••••••••••••••••••••••••••••

Before one puzzle is solved,
life might scramble another.

••••••••••••••••••••••••••••••••

Hopeless Mess?

Has your life seemed like an unsolvable puzzle, possibly with missing pieces? Like Humpty-Dumpty, are you fractured and feel you can never be complete again? Perhaps you have been a victim of crime? Many people see themselves broken or as victims, not sure why they continue living. Most of us have a survival instinct that prevents committing suicide, but despair can reach a point where survival does not seem worth the effort. Hopelessness is a terrible monster.

Look Up and Around

The first attack against hopelessness is to look up (Psalm 5:1-3). Focusing on God instead of personal history, feelings and bad circumstances will eventually lead to breathing fresh air. This is possible only by *making the decision* to do it and to *continue*. God knows all about all and is ready to help, so cry out. One of God's titles is *El Ro'i:* "The God Who sees" (Genesis 16:13). He always knows the precise nature of our circumstances and He wants us to ask Him for help. He loves us so much that He yearns to intervene and rescue us. God is the healer and restorer. Healing is an integral part of His nature.

In addition to looking up, look around to find someone more needy than yourself. Helping others is an antidote to hopelessness, because self-absorption is refocused to addressing other people's difficulties. It causes awareness that others might have it worse than we do, and all have trouble dealing with imperfect worldly social systems. Helping others does not need to be an earthshaking project.

Simple solutions where we live will minister.

The Lord tells us that helping others as led by the Holy Spirit is the same as ministering to Him. Have you heard, "We are human beings, not human "doings"? Being busy helping others just to divert our minds from our problems might be necessary as a start but is, nevertheless, an incorrect motive for earning eternal rewards because of its selfishness. The Lord promises rewards for those who consider the poor (Psalm 41:1), but the necessary ingredients for heavenly rewards are humility and compassion coming only from the Lord. He gives examples for our understanding that doing something good *as led by the Holy Spirit* guarantees heavenly rewards because we will have the proper faith and true compassion (James 2:20-26). That will lift us from the doldrums.

Spiritual Nourishment
If you have had events and situations in your life still keeping you wondering why and what for, just be assured solutions exist. Answers usually come, not swiftly or in complete packages, but in bits and pieces slowly so we can assimilate or digest them.

Isaiah 28:10, describes God's methods: "For precept must be upon precept, precept upon precept, Line upon line, line upon line, Here a little, there a little." Our Lord knows we cannot digest tons of spiritual food at once, so He feeds us baby bites. Incremental learning makes daily Bible reading essential. When I read passages I've read many times and think I know well, the Lord surprises me by bringing things to my attention for clarity and fitting more puzzle pieces into their proper places. For this reason the Bible is called spiritual food, and the Lord Jesus is called the Bread and Water of Life (John 6:35, 51; John 4:14). We can receive complete daily spiritual protein, vitamins and minerals with our hearts in His Word. This occurs when we keep our spiritual eyes and ears open to Him while reading His Word (Ephesians 1:17-20).

Prerequisite to Deep Answers
Gospel writers also differentiated between spiritual baby food and grown-up food (Hebrews 5:13; 1 Peter 2:2). New believers in the Lord must learn basics before deep why questions are answered

about personal experiences. The learning objective is not so much understanding the events as it is recognizing our sinful responses to them, such as unforgiveness, bitterness, depression and more. Accepting responsibility for situations we cause and also making the decision to forgive those responsible for things done to us, enables us to receive the blessings God desires to bestow. It has taken years for me to understand that my sinful responses to past events were just as or more harmful than the events.

My unrighteous responses really were "blotted out," wiped away (Colossians 2:13-14) from my record in heaven when I gave my life to Jesus. He took my judgment upon Himself and set me free. The next step was to retrain my thinking habits with the Word to believe the past is gone, done, covered, cleansed, blotted out, erased, poof!

> When the Lord forgives, He *does not remember our sin* (Isaiah 43:25)! We also must forgive ourselves.

Greatest Issues

Accepting responsibility and forgiving self and others are at the top of a long list of many challenges everyone faces. Forgiveness is a critical and eternal issue, and the Lord's mercy and grace are needed to truly forgive. No one has suffered to the depths that Jesus did, yet He forgave all of them and in the process all of us too. When we are in Him, we have been forgiven mountains of debt. Therefore, He will give us grace to forgive others when we ask. Most people who hurt us truly do not know what they are doing, even if it appears intentional. People who hurt others also hurt themselves.

Forgiveness may seem grossly unfair and even impossible if the suffering has been extreme. Revenge is a normal human reaction but is inexcusable. Forgiveness releases both the perpetrator and the victim to progress toward maturity. However, human beings just cannot be successful in spiritual things with human strength. Only God's love can heal deep wounds. When Jesus Christ, the Messiah is received as Lord and Savior, His Holy Spirit is given with power to forgive, love and live morally and righteously in Him. He has promised to heal and guide us when we ask and listen.

Another super challenge to our maturing in God is to practice listening to Him, because we are so accustomed to hearing our own voices. He can and will speak clearly if we are willing to hear. Ask the Lord to help you hear the Holy Spirit. He promised to open the inner eyes of our understanding to His ways and wisdom and our inner ears to hear His voice (Matthew 13:20-23). You can be sure He hears us when we call to Him (Psalm 94:9).

Restoration, Repair and Replacement

God is in the restoration and repair business but not just piecing us back together like the proverbial thousand piece puzzle that remains individual pieces. He gives us all things new when we are born again (2 Corinthians 5:17). His goal is to cleanse us as if we had never been fractured or strayed from Him. The image on the puzzle box will be past history, replaced by a new and beautiful composition in which all the pieces will be eventually and permanently joined with no fault lines between.

Moral Of The Story

— *Practical lesson:* Practice listening to the Holy Spirit.
— *Spiritual lesson:* Allow time to digest God's spiritual food.

What other lessons might be contained in this devotional?

My Heart

My heart has a door behind which I hide.
The name on the hinges was fear.
The key and the knob are only inside,
And I choose whom I let draw near.
The lock was secure and guarded,
Carefully concealing its contents.
Lonely, in pain and discarded,
A closed heart door my defense.

A knock on the door was expected.
I had asked for help from above.
Knowing I had been detected
As one desperate for love.
The peephole doesn't allow a full view.
I must open to see who or what's there.
The distorted image is only a clue.
Should I open? Do I dare?

Opening the door to my great relief
Was the Messiah, the Christ, my Savior.
He flooded my soul with joy and belief
Cleansing this faulty and damaged chamber.
I've allowed Him to stay on my heart's throne,
Where He directs my coming and going.
My life now is His, I'm not my own,
And He's made me feel I'm worth knowing.

Diane Shields Spears ©

14

Real? Or Fake?

• •

Gold might be just under the surface of "dull."

• •

Prissy was happy and cute as all kittens are but quite ordinary in appearance. Amanda loved to dress her in doll clothes and wheel her around the back yard in a doll stroller. Prissy submitted to the treatment because she loved Amanda. One day when Amanda went inside the house leaving Prissy outside still dressed, a cat

DSS©

Looking Prissy

jumped to the top of the backyard fence and stared at her for several moments. Suddenly this cat began to snicker, then broke out into real guffaws.

Prissy asked timidly, "What's so funny?"

The amused cat sneered, "Do you have any idea how silly and stupid you look? You will be the laughing stock of the entire feline community!" Her tone changed to indignant, "Don't you have any self-respect? I would never allow anyone to do this to me!"

"What's wrong with the way I look?"

"I guess you've never seen yourself in a mirror. Follow me and I'll show you something."

Prissy looked at the house, then still dressed up, made the snap decision to follow this captivating cat. Quickly scrambling out of the stroller she asked, "Hey, what's your name?"

"My human calls me Cecelia. It's just beautiful, don't you think? But I'm just little ol' me with no pretenses." She was not telling the whole truth.

"Well, I think you're stunningly beautiful. I've never seen such bright white hair with red streaks and black around the eyes. What are you going to show me?"

"We're almost there. Hey, what does your human call you?

"Prissy," she responded proudly.

"Good grief! You really have problems! Who would give you a name like that?"

"My little girl named me!" Prissy's tone was defensive.

"Well, we won't change that, but we're here." They entered the back of a building reeking with peculiar odors, tickling Prissy's nose and causing a couple of sneezes. Cecelia spoke in a hushed tone, "Look over here."

Prissy saw a huge wall mirror. Cecelia motioned her to hop on a chair, then onto the counter among curling irons, brushes, combs and spray bottles. Prissy saw herself for the first time.

"Do you see how ridiculous you look?"

Cecelia's opinion started to matter and bewilderment began gnawing. Prissy had never thought about her appearance and was suddenly self-conscious. Then she wondered why someone she loved would do this to her, and began struggling out of the clothes.

Cecelia had to help her strip down to her natural self.

"Now. that's better! Oh my! You're an OK gal, but really quite plain. Let's see what we can do."

At that moment, they heard a sweet greeting from a female voice, "There you are Cecelia. Look what you brought with you. My, aren't you a plain girl! Let's see what we can do," she crooned, repeating Cecelia's comment as if it had been said many times before. The woman scooped up Prissy and stood her in front of the mirror with both their reflections studying the plain girl. "Well, I suppose you have a name because you aren't skinny, so you must belong to someone. I don't suppose your person would mind if we spruced you up a bit. Let's see—uh—your coat is really quite common, so I think we'll put some highlights and streaks in it. Then accentuate your eyes with eyeliner."

Cecelia began to fidget while watching Prissy's transformation.

"There, now. Don't you look just wonderful? Pretty good for a quick job, don't you think, Cecelia?" came the soft voice from the woman. Cecelia gave no acknowledging "meow."

Prissy stood before the mirror and was shocked at the bright blue streaks and eyeliner. She was unsure if she liked it, but the soft voice was gushing admiration about how pretty Prissy had become. Prissy eyed herself again and decided it must be OK, then had a thought, "Will these colors come off?"

"Of course! In fact, you'd better start licking now!" Cecelia's answer was surprisingly curt.

Prissy noticed Cecelia's petulant tone, "What's the matter?"

"I don't like the way you look now at all. In fact, you look more stupid now than before! Why don't you just go home! Go on. I don't want you around anymore! This is my lady and I'm sorry I brought you here!"

Prissy stood stunned at Cecelia's change. "But . . . but I thought we were friends."

"No, we're not friends and I'm the prettiest!"

Prissy jumped down from the counter, took one last look at Cecelia and decided she wanted to go home anyway, sorry that she had let Cecelia influence her. She missed her little girl.

Prissy reached her property, jumped to the fence rail and down into the yard. The stroller was still there, and Amanda sat on the steps crying. The sight made Prissy ache. Prissy confidently approached and meowed softly but Amanda pushed her away. Shocked at the rebuttal, Prissy tried again only to be repelled once more with, "Go on! Go to your own house! I don't want you! I want my Prissy!"

Prissy was crushed that Amanda did not recognize her. She slowly walked away dejected and then hopped onto the stroller and looked at her beloved little girl, hoping this would identify her. Amanda jumped up and screamed, "That belongs to my Prissy! Get out and don't come back!"

Prissy leaped to the ground, jumped back over the fence and wandered aimlessly for several blocks before making a decision. She was now quite self-conscious and avoided being seen. She sat near a bush and began to lick, but the color resisted her tongue and she realized it would take too long. The only immediate solution Prissy could think of was to return to the smelly place for the doll clothes. She was hoping Cecelia or the woman would not be there.

When she arrived, the door was closed and no Cecelia or woman could be heard inside. She was afraid to go through the cat door in case she would be trapped. Dusk was coming. She found a corner to lie down but getting hungry, she decided to jump into the trashcan to look for anything tasty. She landed on a wrapper with part of a hamburger, so that helped. Then she spied the doll clothes. Thrilled, she pulled them out and jumped down to the ground, but she could not dress herself.

Prissy started home with doll clothes in her mouth. Arriving past Amanda's bedtime, she slept on the back porch. In the morning, Amanda emerged from the house and saw Prissy again. She was ready to shout at Prissy when she spied the doll clothes Prissy was lying on. Yanking the doll clothes from under Prissy, she exclaimed loudly, "How did you get these? They belong to my Prissy! What happened to her? What did you do with her?" In her distress, she did not notice blue smears on the doll clothes.

Prissy softly meowed and tried to get her head under Amanda's hand. She withdrew her hand quickly, but Prissy began rubbing her sides on Amanda's legs even though Amanda tried to move her legs away. She then took a long look at Prissy. "Are you Prissy? What happened? Did someone steal you and you got away? Who could do this to you? Are you really Prissy?"

Prissy would not be deterred and continued to rub her sides on Amanda's legs. She looked down to see blue stains on her white socks. Lifting Prissy to her cheek she cooed, "Oh, Prissy! It is you! I'm so glad you are back! How could I be so mean to you! I'm going to give you a bath and get this awful color out of your hair!" Those were love-words to Prissy even though she detested baths.

"I want my Prissy!"

• •

Disguises?

You surely by now have seen the wild hair colors for people. The hair product aisle offers "Splat Hair Rebellious Colors." Among them are "Blue Envy," "Lusty Lavender," and "Pink Fetish." No attempt at looking authentic is mildly refreshing, unlike a bleach job exposed by dark roots, or the elderly pink and blue hair resulting from trying to cover gray or white. The many reasons for changing outwardly include:

— boredom with appearance,

— shock value,
— rebellion—part of the brand name mentioned,
— meeting an acceptable standard of beauty,
— being fashionable,
— looking younger.

All the above reflect dissatisfaction with self. Contrast the lack of pretense of these startling hair colors with implants, heavy make-up and Photoshop adjustments of beauty pageant contestants, models and film stars. False images might also be trying to hide the true inner self. An alluring cultural ideal is placed before us that most of us cannot achieve. Disguising what we consider physical faults does not change the real person inside.

In Hiding

We can deceive ourselves and possibly others into believing we are of greater worth by improving outward appearances, but most outward improvements are temporary and require maintenance. There is nothing wrong with trying to look nice. Be authentic but be the best authentic possible. The wrongness of physical disguises is the reliance on outward appearance as a sign of value instead of concentrating on improving inner qualities. An unwillingness to reveal true character is probably from a subconscious recognition of an imperfect and faulty spiritual state. Focusing on or disguising outward faults will delay or possibly derail desired changes. The solution requires a different focus.

Without Pretense

Prissy was young and inexperienced and was thus easily swayed by Cecelia's opinion without questioning the motive or possible outcome. Likewise, someone popular or attractive can influence our children into wrong thinking. Prissy was told she was a plain girl, and she believed it, especially after hearing it the second time. She forgot her purpose and how important she was to Amanda the way she was. We also tend to forget our purpose and our importance to the Lord. He is the only One able to make changes correctly and permanently. He will begin on the inside aiming for good character, and then those changes will eventually reflect to the outside.

Godly character is infinitely and eternally more important and more beautiful than physical appearance.

Cultural Influence

Hollywood and other glamorous venues play a major role in both swaying and reflecting culture by promoting a "required" standard of beauty and wealth for acceptance. The result can be damaging. Many try to meet that standard and become imposters who lose their identity and sense of purpose.

A strong and seductive social pressure is to amass as much stuff as possible and is universally interpreted as personal value and possibly favored by God. A financial blessing from God is true in some instances. When people please the Lord, He is pleased to bless in many ways, not just monetarily. However, wealth is seductive and will quickly make slaves and destroy good character of those who succumb to its power. Our value to God is not based on our portfolio. That is great news for the majority of us!

Politics also has a strong grip on collective thought, trying to make us think that we must think like others think. A variety of opinions should be allowed in a free society but the winning opinion should be based on correct information. Pride in power is a strong motivation for finding value in this earthly life, but it is not eternal value. God's opinion matters most.

Faulty Me and You

Why are we not perfect? The answer: worldly social systems "fell" from the original perfection as created and have degenerated morally and physically. Since creation, humans have relied on finite mental prowess to fix the world. All human wisdom: science, politics, psychology, religions and a plethora of philosophies have all been offered as solutions, although eternally unsuccessful. These can provide limited and temporary help outwardly but are seldom permanent or valuable unless they lead to a further search for truth. None of these worldly, intellectual strategies are real solutions to the core issues of our imperfections—our full-of-faults condition. Even super human efforts to patch the cracks in personal fault lines can be compared with trying to to patch an old garment with an un-shrunken or unsuitable new piece. Either the garment or the patch will shrink in the wash, and the old garment will tear more (Matthew 9:16-17). Self cannot repair self for eternal benefits.

Past popular bracelets contained the *alphabetism* PBPGIFWMY. The meaning: "Please be patient; God isn't finished with me yet." He has a plan for ultimately and permanently removing personal fault lines. Another popular adage was "Still under construction." Cooperating 100 percent with His remodeling projects in us will bring joy.

Begin With Milk

Let the Living Word of God (the Lord Jesus) and the written word (Scripture) do the repairs. Remember, the Holy Spirit teaches little by little, so patience is crucial. No one becomes instantly mature without spot or wrinkle (Ephesians 5:27). Those with true spiritual hunger will grasp the easily digested basics called the "milk of the Word," ("baby bites") (Hebrews 5:12-13). Milk basics understanding comes by reading and believing the Gospels (the first four books of the New Testament). The "meat" of God's Word is deeper and requires continued study. Solid spiritual food in the entire Bible will provide a complete nutritious spiritual diet. You will learn so much more about our wonderful Savior, Who will draw you closer in the process.

The Lord always tests us to demonstrate if we are serious about our relationship with Him. He already knows if we are or are not serious, but it must be revealed to us, because sometimes intentions are subconsciously substituted for real commitment. When a serious commitment is made to follow the Lord, digesting the meat of the Word begins. God loves our searching for Him and rewards us with understanding and joy in His presence. He searches for us!

Persistent Fault Lines

Our inherent faulty condition sometimes hinders receiving God's love. Fault lines in our personalities can interfere with fulfilling His entire plan for us individually. The Lord wants to deal with all the fault lines so He can reward us on Earth and in Heaven. He has the best "first aid kit"—the Holy Spirit and the Word of God. His goal is to bless us beyond our imaginations (Ephesians 3:20).

True Value

When we realize how immensely valuable we are to God, we will not be consumed with what we consider deficiencies, or defects. We are fearfully and wonderfully made individuals (Psalm 139:1-18). The inner being—our essence—the heart (the human soul and spirit)—is the most important part, regardless of inherited physical flaws, low or average IQ's or talent deficiencies. Again, God does an inside job before it shows on the outside.

Each person is truly one of a kind even if a look-alike. The soul is unique and precious. We are not supposed to look or be exactly like others. No other *you* exists in the entire universe! God loves variety. Look at the variety of butterflies. Scientists have documented 15-20,000 species and are not certain all have been discovered.[1] In addition, variations in the species and in the entire creation seem limitless.

A New Image

God's main purpose for our lives is to be conformed to the image of our Lord Jesus Christ, *Yeshua* the Messiah (Romans 8:29; 12:2). He will correct flaws that interfere when we submit to His construction plan. Each earthly life finds true value and purpose(s) only in a relationship with Him.

Moral Of The Story

— *Practical lesson:* God's opinion of you matters most. You are of great worth to Him.
— *Spiritual lesson:* Find the real you in the Lord Jesus, the Gentile Christ, the Jewish Messiah.

What other lessons might be contained in this parable?

---

1. *The World Book Encyclopedia.* 1991. s.v. "Butterfly."

Fault Lines

Cracks in the globe,
Destruction potential,
Situations to probe,
Consequences plural.
Our substance is earth,
Various faults,
Cracks in our worth—
Embedded defaults.
Ruptures in souls,
Personal quake,
Detours from goals
While we shake.
Longing for peace,
Falling on knees,
Seeking release,
Shown the keys.
Answers found,
Cracks healed,
Change profound,
Judgment repealed.

Diane Shields Spears ©

15

The Tree Amigos

....
Maturity is a necessary burden.
....

Three very good pals continually raced each other through the trees so fast they were almost a blur. This fun loving bunch of young squirrels was seldom serious. Frolicking in the warm air and sunshine, the three scurried toward the familiar blaring sound of Saturday morning cartoons and comedies and scampered up a vine to their observation seats in a window flower box. Sitting among the flowers, they were enthralled and inspired, backslapping, chattering and laughing uproariously over an Our Gang/The Little Rascals Comedy re-run. The TV volume masked their noise.

"Our Gang is really funny!"

Swinging back into the trees at the conclusion, they excitedly huddled together in a powwow to discuss how to be like the Rascals.

"I know! We all need nicknames," chattered Roscoe, then quickly added, "Hey, let's choose a name for our gang too!" Theodore and

Clarence agreed, racing around the tree trunk, hardly able to contain their enthusiasm before settling back down. Clarence teased, "I think Theodore should be called Teddy."

"Good grief! That sounds like a fluffy plump toy! That's not me at all!" objected Theodore but with twinkling eyes. Pausing only for a moment, he chuckled, "How 'bout this for a gang name—the Cut-Up Gang?' We've been called a bunch of cut-ups."

"It sounds dangerous to add the word gang to cut-up," cautioned Roscoe. They spent a few rare moments in silence.

"How 'bout The Nutty Gang?" Theodore was always on the spot with ideas.

"I don't like that one," Clarence protested emphatically. "I mean it kind-a describes us 'cause we like nuts and seeds, but it sounds too crazy, even for us."

"Well, it might be easier to think of nicknames for us," suggested Roscoe. "They need to be sort-a descriptive of us but not mean or stupid."

Clarence instantly suggested name for Theodore—*Fuzzy Face*, or *Fuzzy* for short.

Theodore only mildly objected, because he knew it was true and his friends were good-natured. "As long as that doesn't refer to my brain!" The others laughed. "But it's OK." Fuzzy stuck.

Fuzzy then proposed *Speedy* for Clarence who immediately objected stating that they were all exceptionally speedy and that the name sounded too much like a cartoon character they had enjoyed watching through the window.

They thought for a moment again in unaccustomed silence before Fuzzy spoke again, "OK, how 'bout *Leaper* for Clarence? I mean he's better than us (pointing to Roscoe and himself) at leaping from tree to tree. He can leap further than we can."

"Yeah, that fits! Leaper it is!" Clarence was pleased.

Roscoe still needed a new name. They thought and thought and thought, and were again unnaturally quiet for an unnatural amount of time for naturally squirrelly beings. They finally realized it was time to go home to their respective moms.

"See ya in the morning," they hollered at each other as they dashed through the trees.

The next day, a name for Roscoe came from observing his favorite method of grabbing the delectable sunflower seeds. A bird feeder hung from a tree limb approximately twelve inches from the nearest tree trunk and was continuously refilled with seeds. Roscoe became *Stretch,* not because he is long-bodied, but because he could stretch like a rubber band. They teased him that stretching from the tree trunk, grasping with hind feet, throwing his body into the air to grab the feeder platform with front feet and exposing his underbelly is undignified. It became hilarious when one hind foot lost its hold, waving around in the air. Their good-natured teasing did not deter him. He liked his new nickname.

Fuzzy and Leaper were just as humorous in their quest for bird seed. They always made the bird feeder swing and whirl by its one chain when they landed on it, then had to be still for a moment until their heads stopped spinning before they were able to get to the seed. Fuzzy's strategy was to hang from the roof peak by his hind

Seed Gathering Styles

toes to reach the seed on the platform. Leaper jumped directly to the platform swaying Fuzzy and reached over the rim with one front paw to get the seed. The rest of him was swinging freely in the air. Leaper's method certainly looked the most difficult. When Stretch saw their strategies, he returned their laughter. The three friends had much fun.

The friends still had not decided on a gang name. Suddenly aware of the TV noise, they clambered to the window box. *The Three Amigos* movie thoroughly entertained them. After the movie, they raced through the trees expending energy and ended at their favorite spot to rest a moment. They discussed how much fun the movie was. Suddenly Fuzzy, who was always full of fun ideas, exclaimed excitedly, "I've got it! I've got it! I know what we should call our gang—the *Tree Amigos*!"

Eyes widened and jaws dropped in astonishment at the brilliance of this name.

"That's it! That's it!" Stretch and Leaper again chased each other exuberantly around the trunk with Fuzzy grinning from ear to ear, impressed with his inspiration.

The Tree Amigos Gang became well known among all the tree dwellers—raccoons, all birds and of course other squirrels. Some creatures became exasperated with the Tree Amigos' antics, but most were able to ignore them. The three seemed to be majoring in fun, fun and more fun.

Eventually, the Tree Amigos' mothers and other tree dwellers became weary of the constant laughing, chattering and innocent cut-ups. It seemed as if the Tree Amigos were incapable of being serious about anything. The mothers attempted to keep them in the nests until later in the morning to give the birds first chance at the seeds. It worked only one day. The Tree Amigos were too active for the nests.

Other squirrels wanted membership in the Tree Amigos Gang. This idea was rejected because the three had a camaraderie that no one else could understand, and the others were no fun besides. The rejection of increasing membership in the Tree Amigos was met with sneers, vilification and then ignoring their presence.

Competition was inevitable. Last year's conceited BMOC,

Chuck, suggested to his buddies, Samson and Abe, "There's no reason why we can't start our own gang! What duh ya say?"

"We're definitely superior," remarked Samson who was really thickheaded and clumsy.

"We could start recruiting the first day of school. There'd be more of us," Abe reasoned.

"Good idea!" chorused Chuck and Samson.

Chuck added, "Should we think of a gang name now?"

"Why not? Got'ny ideas?" asked Samson.

"Well . . . " Chuck's voice trailed off. "Let's see, we could think of some things we like as a start. We all like birdseed, acorns, nuts, figs and such. How 'bout Acorns-R-Us?"

Something did not seem quite right about that suggestion. They were silent again for a while. Samson, desperately wanting to appear intelligent, piped up, "How 'bout The Brainy Group?" This was also rejected as being a little too haughty even for them.

"What about The Tree Nuts?" suggested Abe. A long moment of silence followed while they contemplated the title. He continued, "Nah, that one's not quite it. It's too close to the other gang name." Another moment of silence ensued.

"I know!" shouted Chuck enthusiastically, the *Nut Clusters*! That sounds like a gang that likes nuts!"

"Gee, you're really clever, Chuck. I like that one," replied Abe turning to Samson. "Don't you like it?"

"Sure. I think it's inspired. Chuck is really smart."

"Are we going to let just anybody join?" asked Abe.

"Why not?" replied Chuck and added, "We'd have the majority over the Tree Amigos. Besides, the girls'll probably want to join us 'cause we're more popular and better-looking."

The one-classroom school began to the delight of the squirrel parents who were tired by the end of summer of corralling their little ones. The Nut Clusters were able to recruit almost all the students and considered themselves in charge of the student body. They also believed they were the teacher's favorites, because they were more serious and paid attention in class.

The Tree Amigos were outnumbered but not outsmarted. They sat at the back of the classroom constantly communicating in stage whispers and cutting up, but when asked questions of the lessons, they gave correct answers. They only looked like they were not listening. Their dramatic whispering and cut-ups distracted the more serious students, producing faltering and occasionally wrong answers. Frowns were frequent on embarrassed faces.

"Why don't you guys just shut up!" burst out Sally Mae, the Nut Clusters' sweetheart.

The teacher, Miss Winifred, whacked a pecan on her desk for attention, cracking it into several pieces. She took time to eat the pieces before speaking, keeping her wide-eyed class in suspense. She finally spoke, "If you don't cut out this racket, you'll be given detention!" The Tree Amigos knew if that happened, they would be in a heap of trouble at home, so they quieted down and frowned at Sally Mae. It was fortunate only a few minutes remained of class time or they would have burst.

After class, the Nut Clusters confronted the Tree Amigos. "Hey, tree dopes, you'd better not mess with us, if you know what's good for you," threatened Chuck. Stretch, Fuzzy and Leaper dramatized fear, prompting giggles from the Nut Clusters' girls. The three blinked their eyes in astonishment. They had thought no girls would ever like them, and they raced away through the trees with extra energy. When they reached their favorite place, they strategized.

"What would make the girls want to join us?" asked Fuzzy.

"Why don't we gather as many sunflower seeds as we can and offer them to the girls at school tomorrow?" That was a big sacrifice for Stretch since sunflower seeds were the main reason he stretched from the tree limb to the bird feeder. Fuzzy and Leaper understood the sacrifice and offered to help collect them. They set to work as soon as they saw the TV owner put more seed in the feeder.

The next day before school they looked for the clump of girls who always hung together, including Sally Mae. The Amigos were reluctant to give Sally Mae any seed since she had been mean to them in class the day before. They approached the girls anyway with the seeds wrapped in a huge fig leaf.

"Hi girls," saluted Stretch, Fuzzy and Leaper but not in unison, making their greeting sound like an echo.

"Hi yourself!" was the semi-unfriendly answer.

"Hey, we brought some sunflower seeds for you gals. Duh ya want some?" asked Stretch, glancing defiantly at Chuck.

"Sure. Thanks," they replied as they all began munching. The girls said nothing more to the Tree Amigos and when finished with the seeds, went to class.

The Nut Clusters leaders had been watching. Anger was rising and they were determined to get even. After class, they confronted the girls and warned them about bribes, announcing they were permanent members of the Nut Clusters. The Clusters were not quick enough to challenge the Tree Amigos again this time, as the Amigos had skedaddled after class to avoid any confrontation.

Back in their favorite spot, the Amigos ridiculed the rival gang. "Ya know they're not even smart enough to give themselves nicknames. We could do that for them, couldn't we?"

"Yeah!" They snickered and became unnaturally quiet for an unnatural moment for naturally squirrelly creatures.

A big grin began to spread on Fuzzy's face. "Hey, Chuck could be—*Up-Chuck*," he suggested, trying his best to speak clearly while beginning to laugh. They all roared and rolled with laughter until tears streamed and stomach muscles ached.

"Samson could be, let's see—*Muscle Head*!" Becoming weak with laughter, all they could do was double over and stomp feet.

"Abe could be . . ." began Leaper.

Rustling leaves overhead interrupted. The Nut Clusters had heard their glee and were descending upon them.

"Don't you dare try to take our members! They're not yours!" shouted Chuck menacingly with a disfiguring frown.

"What-cha gunna do 'bout it?" challenged Stretch. "They're free to choose what they want."

"No they aren't! They belong to us and you can't have them! They are permanent members of the Nut Clusters," threatened Abe, standing tall with outstretched fist.

"You can't own them!" protested Stretch in astonishment.

"Oh yes we can! And—we already do! So leave 'em alone!" At that, the Nut Clusters made a synchronized turn and raced way as if the matter were settled.

"Well!" puffed Stretch when they were gone. "What about

that? We can't just let this drop! Those poor girls don't know they will become slaves if we don't do something. The guys aren't speaking up for them." They had viewed a news report from their window flower box of little girls becoming slaves. This was one of the few serious moments for them.

"Got'ny ideas?" asked Fuzzy.

"We're going to have to think hard about this. It might be the hardest thing we will do in our short lives, but I feel strongly about it." Stretch paused a moment. "You remember the TV news report, don't you? It looks like it could happen here in the trees. We just have to do something. Do you see the danger?"

"Don't you think you are *stretching* things out of proportion?" punned Fuzzy with a grin.

Leaper chuckled but stated seriously, "No, I think Stretch is on to something here and sensing some real danger. Just think for a minute. We didn't have any trouble in the trees till we started our gang. now we have some real unhealthy competition. And our cut-ups and pranks might have contributed to their annoyance with us. I know our parents and Miss Winifred would agree. Do you think maybe we are still immature? I know we have to grow up sometime, but I haven't wanted to till now. I thought Peter Pan had a good idea."

"All fantasy, fantasy," stated Fuzzy, "but probably we've been obsessed with having fun. That's going to be a severe hardship on us to change."

"Golly. I don't really want to change. Give up racing? That's too much to ask," retorted Leaper, dismayed at the possibility.

"We don't have to give up racing—maybe just our cut-ups. I'll bet Miss Winifred would appreciate that. Maybe we can be quieter in school knowing we can still race after."

Leaper added, "We'll sure need to race if we can manage to be quiet in school." Heads nodded in agreement.

The next day at school the Tree Amigos chose new seats so they would not be tempted to whisper and cut-up. Miss Winifred was in awe of their silence but pleased, asking, "Are you three OK?" Their chorused, enthusiastic answer, "Yes'm," silenced her for a moment before continuing the lesson.

At the end of class, Miss Winifred called the Tree Amigos to her desk. The Clusters snickered and decided to hang around to see how much trouble the Amigos were in. She waited until everyone else had left the class before speaking. "I'm very pleased you acted like you paid attention today. I realize you have abilities to learn while many other things are going on, because you answer questions in class accurately. I don't pretend to know how you do that, but I understand not everyone has that ability. So, I just wanted you to know you helped the others in the class today, and I want to encourage you to keep it up. It really can be satisfying and a lot of fun helping others."

The Tree Amigos stood stunned for a moment. "Thanks, Miss Winifred. This wasn't easy, but we'll keep trying."

Outside, the Clusters were ready with their ridicule. Chuck spoke first, " Hey, goof nuts, did Miss Winifred finally give you the detention you deserve?"

"Actually, no," replied Stretch calmly with a smile.

"Sure she did!" contradicted Abe. "You just won't admit it!"

"No, she really didn't," confirmed Stretch. "We may be cut-ups, but we tell the truth."

"What happened in there, then?" persisted Samson.

"That's between Miss Winifred and us," Stretch wisely replied. "But we want to tell you guys and gals we're sorry for annoying you. We really don't want to compete with you. We don't want to be a rival gang."

"Yeah, you know you'll lose, that's why," retorted Chuck.

"It has never mattered to us who wins or loses, 'cause we know none of us are good at everything. We just wanted to have fun. Our decision to tone it down in class was not forced on us."

"I'll bet!" sneered Chuck. "I'll bet she threatened to expel you, and you'd be in big trouble at home." Abe and Samson nodded in agreement. The other classmates huddled in the background.

"No," calmly stated Stretch, trying to be patient. "We decided to ask all of you to join us. We're not even going to call it a gang any more. We don't need to be against each other, so let's make peace. We can be friends—all of us if you want. In fact, did you know that *amigos* really means friends?"

"I want to be friends," muttered Carol shyly. "Me too." "I do too," piped up several girls.

"Yeah, I'm tired of this gang stuff anyway," remarked Leon. Ralph and several others stepped forward with him. "Me too." "Me too." It was catching on.

"I don't think I'm hearing right," stated Chuck sternly, believing he was still in control. "If you leave the Nut Clusters now, you will never be allowed in again." Abe, Samson, and Sally Mae stood by him with resolute faces.

"Everybody's welcome," confirmed Fuzzy. We weren't enemies before. Let's all be friends—be Amigos."

Carol found boldness, "I want to be an Amigo. I don't want to be told I can't leave a gang if I want to!"

Everyone except Chuck, Samson, Abe, and Sally Mae actually moved bodily over to the original three Amigos. They all began chattering excitedly.

Chuck shouted spitefully, "Whatever! I don't care what you do! You can't come back again! Ever!"

"We don't want to! Bye!" All the new Tree Amigos excitedly followed the original three through the trees to the widest and longest horizontal limb in the woods, where they waited for Stretch to speak.

"I'm glad you decided to come with us. We were really worried about you gals not being free. You will be free with us; in fact, we'll protect you." Stretch sounded quite masculine and protective, feeling courageous and encouraged by their support. "We still like to race, but we never get mad if we lose or get prideful if we win. If you can be a friend like that, you are welcome indeed."

"Sounds good to me," stated Linda, the prettiest squirrel. "We haven't been allowed hardly out of their sight since the Clusters was formed. It feels good to be free! I'd like to race again. I've never been really fast but I enjoy it."

"Let's go then!" The original three took off like a shot with most of the new Amigos following. They could be heard all through the trees, causing all the mothers to poke their heads out of hollow trees and over nest edges to enjoy the spectacle. They finally came to rest at the favorite place again."

Stretch spoke, "Day after tomorrow is Saturday and so we'd like to show you something special. Would everyone meet here at 8:30 Saturday morning?"

"Sure!" Excitement was growing.

"OK. See ya in class tomorrow then."

The next day many bright shiny faces contrasting with four sour ones sat at their stations in front of Miss Winifred. She was aware of all the events and had been praying for them all. The four Nut Clusters, realizing they had lost their control, remained sullen throughout the entire day. After class, the Amigos invited the four remaining Clusters to the "something special" that was going to happen the next morning. Sneering, they declined hearing anything about it and took off in their exclusive little group, heads held high.

The next morning all Tree Amigos met at the favorite place, and all chattered with excitement. Stretch led the way to the hanging feeder first. He explained they knew the feeder would hold three at a time, but could not guarantee a fourth would not break the chain. He, Leaper, and Fuzzy demonstrated their hanging feeder styles, sparking much laughter and joy. He warned that all would need to share. The new members were awe-struck at the feeder, exclaiming they did not have anything like that where they lived. Stretch then motioned toward the familiar TV noise. They climbed the flowery trellis and arranged themselves. It was a little crowded, but the guys didn't mind being cozy with the gals.

A program caught their attention. Stretch excitedly shouted, "This is the movie that inspired us to form the Tree Amigos in the first place!" Laughter and giggles were sure signs they were having fun. The remaining four stubborn Nut Clusters had followed them from a distance and had climbed a nearby tree overlooking the flower box. A good view of the program was obstructed by reflections off the window.

"They invited us to join them. Do you think we would still be welcome?" asked Samson hopefully.

"I dunno," replied the still sullen Chuck. "I'm not gunna try."

"Well, I am," stated the now independent Abe. "I believe their invitation was sincere."

"Yeah. Come on, Chuck. At least let's find out."

"You go ahead." He stubbornly added, "I'll just sit here with Sally Mae." Abe and Samson worked their way to the flower box.

United at Last

"But I want to go too," insisted Sally Mae.

"No. Absolutely not! You sit here with me!"

Sally Mae looked long and hard at Chuck. "I guess the Amigos were right about you! I've been such a fool! You just want to control us so you feel more important! Well, I'm going with them to that window box, and you just try and stop me!"

Chuck shouted, "Whatever!" causing a few heads in the window box to turn in his direction with "Shush!"

"Come on down, Chuck," hollered Abe. This is a lot of fun! They're not gunna fight you ur nuthin'! Come on!"

"I'll just sit here for a while," he stated, still unwilling to yield. He tried to watch, but the reflection of the trees in the window was frustrating. Finally, he swallowed his pride and silently eased down from the tree limb to the vine and up to the window box where he was enthusiastically welcomed. Chuck let himself have fun for the first time in a long time.

• •

Acceptable and Unacceptable

Do you know anyone like Chuck? Bullies can operate from pride but normally feel inadequate and devalued. Bullying can take many forms and all contain abuse. Patience, forgiveness and love are required when dealing with a bully. The roots of bullying are deep and love is often vehemently resisted because of disbelief that anyone could love them. Dealing with a bully requires God's *agape* love—the love that only comes from Him and the only love that could minister to both the bully and the recipient. Human generated love can fall tragically short.

Sharing is not a built-in automatic response for humanity and is more easily learned early in life. Continued or unbridled selfishness brings much inner and outer turmoil and can lead to bullying and *manipulation*—a prime ingredient in bullying.

The Tree Amigos could have understandably refused to invite Chuck as retribution for his competitive and mean behavior. Although they welcomed him, it took much convincing before Chuck believed it. Chuck had an inflated ego that can cause social difficulties. The Amigos could have been bitter, unforgiving and vengeful, making the situation worse. Instead, the Amigos shared, knowing the hanging feeder was a fun experience. They spoke a silent message that everyone is important and valued.

Authority? Or Manipulation?

Who is the boss? Some people are ordained by God to have legal authority over others. Parents must control and teach underage children, bosses can tell employees how to work, teachers must have charge of the class for learning to take place, laws must be observed and more. Unless we have God-given or legal authority, we have none.

However, a wide difference exists between legal authority and manipulation. A manipulator attempts to bend someone's will to his or her preference (selfishness) through sneaky or blatant intimidation. It can happen in a context of legal authority as in married spouses selfishly manipulating each other. Children try it on parents. The success of manipulation thrives in an atmosphere of fear. The bully *manipulates from fear through fear to fear.*

Manipulation is not love. A description of the kind of love God wants us to practice is clearly delineated in First Corinthians chapter thirteen. The person with legal authority has the right to control, but must administer it with love and respect.

The Lord has the legal right to tell us what to do, because He created us. Thereafter, we have the free will to either obey or disobey. God never manipulates. God continues to give us the freedom to destroy ourselves if we insist. He loves, He woos, He gives us the information we need to be on His winning side, but we still have the choice to receive or reject.

Far Fetched Example

This story presents squirrels that are quite advanced which, of course, they are not. However, many people are not advanced, either. The Amigos suddenly matured from just having fun and thinking of themselves to understanding how they affected those around them. Behavior that brings peace reveals a higher level of maturity. However, most of us do not suddenly come to an advanced understanding on our own.

Remember Miss Winifred had been praying for them? Never dismiss or underestimate the power of prayer. God works in us from the inside out through the leading of the Holy Spirit and obedience to His guidance. Praying for others is like the final click in unlocking God's power. God does what we cannot do. We all need people to pray for us and they need us to pray for them.

Peace Keeping Versus Peace Making

A vast gulf exists between keeping peace and making peace. A peace-keeper keeps conflict at bay through compromise that is more difficult and normally unsuccessful for permanence. By contrast, a peacemaker tells the truth even if it disturbs the peace for a while. Jesus, the Prince of Peace, stated that He did not come (while on Earth the first time) to make peace (Matthew 10:34). He was warning that commitment to Him could cause trouble between family members, friends and the world, but that we should not let that deter us from administering truth with love about God. The ultimate outcome of the Lord Jesus' life and ministry will be peace for the entire universe after His Second Coming when He reigns as King on Earth for a thousand years—first term.

The Tree Amigos ruffled the fur of the Nut Clusters for a short time before there was resolution—usually a lengthy process if change is resisted. Truth will win if persistently offered without compromise. Patience, forgiveness, love and truth that work by God's higher love are the characteristics of a peacemaker.

Unworthy? Or Worthy?

We are all special creations of God, and He cares deeply for each of us. As mentioned before, there is no one else in the universe exactly like you—*there is no other you*. The Lord Jesus informed us of our value in the New Testament Book of Luke:

> 6 Are not five sparrows sold for two copper coins? And not one of them is forgotten before God.
> 7 But the *very hairs of your head are all numbered.* Do not fear therefore; *you are of more value than many sparrows.* (Luke 12:6-7, emphasis added).

Do you know now many hairs are on your head? God knows all and cares about every detail of our lives. All creation is important to Him, but He has placed special value on people as being eligible for true and deep fellowship with Him in His presence.

When we come into this world, we are not worthy to come into God's presence because of humanity's inherited fault lines of sin. However, we are not a lost cause, because the Lord Jesus' life was given for us as the remedy—our substitute in death for punishment we deserve.

The following verses provide additional comfort, confirming how special people are to the Lord.

> 22 Then He said to His disciples, "Therefore I say to you, do not worry about your life, what you will eat; nor about the body, what you will put on.
> 23 Life is more than food, and the body is more than clothing.
> 24 Consider the ravens, for they neither sow nor reap, which

have neither storehouse nor barn; and God feeds them. Of how much more value are you than the birds?

25 And which of you by worrying can add one cubit to his stature?

26 If you then are not able to do the least, why are you anxious for the rest?

27 Consider the lilies, how they grow: they neither toil nor spin; and yet I say to you, even Solomon in all his glory was not arrayed like one of these.

28 If then God so clothes the grass, which today is in the field and tomorrow is thrown into the oven, how much more will He clothe you, O you of little faith?

29 And do not seek what you should eat or what you should drink, nor have an anxious mind.

30 For all these things the nations of the world seek after, and your Father knows that you need these things.

31 But seek the kingdom of God, and all these things shall be added to you.

32 Do not fear, little flock, for it is your Father's good pleasure to give you the kingdom (Luke 12:22-32).

Despite the fact that each person is unique and highly valued by God, that alone is not enough to make us pleasing to Him. We come to God only His Way, His terms and not ours, because He is the only Door to the kingdom of heaven—His presence.

Moral Of The Story

— *Practical lesson:* Look for humor and be willing to laugh at yourself.

— *Spiritual lesson:* Forgiveness along with understanding of our personal value to God releases us from bondage and heals wounds.

What other lessons might be contained in this parable?

··· 16 ···

Fourth Dimension

Time is a gift, so use it wisely.

Time is a relative phenomenon—a subject profoundly addressed by Einstein and successors. Scientifically, it is referred to as *space-time*. The "Camping Stuff" anecdote proposed one of the greatest benefits of changing routines was the perception that *time was fuller* —"expanded" to include more content and significance. Time was still scientifically measurable, but more moments were not lost from consciousness or emotions.

Some Negatives

Time is valuable, of course. Myriads of time-saving devices have been invented since harnessing electricity and have placed western societies on a fast track—to where? Most inventions save time and sweat, but are they all beneficial for our wellbeing?

Many time-savers produce anxiety in subtle ways by crowding time with more content devoid of meaningful emotion. In addition, entertainment (amusement) has been gradually replacing analytical, independent thinking. The Greek word *muse* means "to think," and the prefix *a-* means "not." Is that definition surprising or *amusing*? So much time thinking on the wrong things or not thinking at all interferes with proper preparation for what the "olive press" of life might throw our way. Therefore, logical thinking on important issues plus having identifiable, strong, purposeful goals is vital in using time wisely.

"Getting ahead" can become an obsession while robbing quality time spent with family or friends. Stories circulate about people who spent their entire lives working twelve to sixteen hours a day only to lose their health and/or family. Some people escape into entertainment as a symptom of not knowing thier purpose and become immobilized by an inability to cope with life pressures. Near the end of life, they would probably want to freeze or extend time for "do-overs." All of us might wish for that occasionally. Not filling our time with meaningful activities or not understanding the purpose for using that time could bring despair, giving up or other destructive behavior.

Working for a living of course takes major chunks of time, so it is a tremendous blessing if the work is enjoyable. The emotional and mental content will be stimulating and make moments count. If the job is just for the paycheck, it can become drudgery unless there are specific high goals for that income. Goals of advancement in business hierarchy only for money or status includes the risk of succumbing to unhealthy competition and devaluing the rungs (other people) on the ladder. Both money and pride are empty treasure chests spiritually, mentally, emotionally and physically.

The Blessing of Time

I have been greatly blessed to earn a living with art—a subject many consider only a hobby. However, during my first college year, my parents advised and finally convinced me that I should get a teaching certificate to fall back on in case of personal economic collapse. That was parental wisdom but also acceptable, because I had wanted to be a teacher since the third grade.

While teaching combined fifth-sixth grade classes in a Christian school, I began incorporating art into the prescribed curriculum to make academics appealing and significant for all. Writing art curriculum was so enjoyable that I realized it was a strength—a new goal for creating art. Through continued research, I learned of the tremendous benefits art plays in children's brain development and every aspect of the process was interesting. I found my niche and I give God the credit. Through my experience, I learned that the Lord takes much time and many routes of training to arrive at an individual's purpose. This makes daily fellowship with Him crucial for staying on the right path.

When Time Feels Slow

So, what is the solution to feeling stuck in dreariness that seems a waste of time? On the other hand, are you wondering what to do with your time? Specific directions will be individual, but attitude is universally the same and gravely important. I am not special. I just worked hard and did not give up in the rough and tough times. My attitude had to change from defeat to winning, but I did not do this all on my own, and *it was not instant*. I did, however, need to make the decision to do what was necessary. I had help and guidance from the Lord to find my calling. That is the way you will find yours too (Jeremiah 29:11-14). I truly believe the Lord has a plan for each individual life that is absolutely a perfect fit. This normally does not mean easy, but you will reap rewards for sticking with it.

Use your valuable time to seek the Lord about your interests and the areas where you excel. Consider limiting TV time (amusement!) and visits to social web sites. Keeping in touch with people is quite important but avoid letting it become obsessive.

Fading Flowers

Considering eternity without end, our lives on Earth are "brief and full of trouble" (Job 14:1). The length of human life is described as "grass that withers and flowers that fade (Psalm 103: 15)." Every person on this planet has troubles—"God makes His sun to shine on the evil and on the good, and sends rain on the just and the unjust (Matthew 5: 45)." That is, God does not target us for tribulations. We live in a world that is not functioning as originally designed. In addition, we have a spiritual mortal enemy who targets us (1 Peter 5:8). Our attitude toward and strategies to deal with troubles and opposition will determine how we live our relatively brief life and if we will be a winner over less than perfect circumstances. Will we confront difficulties with consistent daily prayer or escape into amusement?

Rewards in Time

Everyone has wasted time on things with no eternal value, but this is not a condemnation requiring the avoidance of all hobbies or recreation. Everyone needs a variety of tasks and activities for good mental and physical health. However, non-eternal moments cannot be reclaimed. God measures pursuits from an eternal reward perspective, and those not led by the Holy Spirit can be what the Bible calls "works"—human ideas of "doing good." Therefore, *the inspiration (the idea's source), purpose and manner in which pursuits are conducted* relates to the issue of eternal rewards.

Redeeming Time

The word *redeem* is used to apply credit to something. For example, we redeem coupons while shopping. Scripture uses the term in two divergent but related connotations:

— buying back, as in we are redeemed from destruction by the sacrifice and shed blood of the Lord Jesus,
— making eternal use of time.

We often refer to using time as spending it. Therefore, spending time is an investment in our future whether positive or negative. Time can only be redeemed in spending it for eternal purposes (Ephesians 5:16). We absolutely cannot do this without the leading of the Holy Spirit, or it would be self-effort (works), worthless and without rewards (1 Corinthians 3:6-15). We can redeem, or buy back future moments by doing first things first. What would a list of "first things first" look like?

— daily prayer; ask God to show you Who He Is.
— Bible reading and study; ask God to teach you.
— Let God's Holy Spirit guide you in every detail; *i.e. let Him use your time in all pursuits.*

Therefore, do what needs to be done to fellowship with the Lord—first. Mundane daily activities can be made a part of worship when remaining aware of God's presence, praying audibly or silently and doing the best job possible. Then continue your attitude of praise and thanksgiving in all your activities. Your spent time can have eternal value and may even feel extended.

A Magnificent Gift

Time given at birth is not earned but is simply by God's grace—a gift to be treasured. Temporal items will rust, spoil or perish, so a primary goal of acquiring stuff or prestige is a waste of this precious gift. The Lord's grace guides our development over time to fulfill our specially designed purpose. His plans are more than marvelous and could include wealth with the directive to bless others. God's higher plan for wealth is more than mere accumulation for selfish use. His plan for you promises the joy and fulfillment you seek.

Reciprocating

God does not need my money or stuff, although He directs me to give so He can bless me. He owns it all (Psalm 50:10). What He does not own once freely given at birth are the individual's time allotments. His gift of time also comes with complete freedom to choose how it is spent. Since He has freely given me my time on Earth, it is mine, not His, unless I give it back to Him. That is the only offering I can give Him that really counts.

When we spend time on a project or with a person, we are really investing ourselves. Therefore, giving ourselves is the ultimate gift the Lord really wants. Pretend it is Christmas, and all He wants for Christmas is you and some of your time in fellowship with Him.

My attitude now is that I'm going to live the time it takes to either make life satisfying or not, so I might as well use my time wisely cooperating with the Holy Spirit's perfect guidance.

What will you choose—to waste time in amusement or redeem it? Spending time on eternal matters as led by the Holy Spirit will build treasure that really counts—that honors the Lord.

Moral Of The Story
  — *Practical lesson:* Identify what you do well and like best.
    Never give up!
  — *Spiritual lesson:* Spent time cannot be reversed, but future
    time can be redeemed by focusing your energy on eternal
    things as led by the Holy Spirit.

What other lessons might be suggested in this devotional?

Enemy? Or Friend?

Wispy grays driven in haste
Across azure finely shaded
Resemble smoke and scurry of waste
Motion—reminding me of faded
Moments of inspiration—
The metaphor they present.
With yesterday's awareness and appreciation,
Swiftly moving clouds have meant
The passage of time gained or lost.
Can I organize my thoughts and pace
To forget and nullify the cost
Of time irretrievably lost in space?
What about the time I spend?
Is time my enemy or friend?

My heart in rhythm with the clocks,
Paid no attention to the place
Of emptiness that now mocks,
Regret for foolish waste.
Is life about accomplishment?
Does every moment have direction?
Or is it merely accident
That what appears to be diversion
Contains elements of timelessness?
My sense of urgency and worry
Contradict aimlessness,
But necessitate blur and flurry.
What about the time I spend?
Is time my enemy or friend?

Diane Shields Spears ©

Apples and Doctors

••••••••••••••••••••••••••••••

Misunderstanding by some can be prophesied.

••••••••••••••••••••••••••••••

Shortly after dinner, our four-year-old son asked for a snack. I told him he could have the half apple left in the refrigerator.

"But, Mom," he protested dramatically, "I already had an apple today. Why do I *always* have to eat an apple *every* day?"

"Because they're good for you," I replied. "A famous proverb says, 'An apple a day keeps the doctor away.'"

He was silent for a moment, wrinkled his forehead and asked, "Keep the doctor away—why? Don't they like apples?"

•••••••••••••••••••••••••••••••

When you are misunderstood, is it worth a chuckle or is it serious? Literal interpretations by children can be delightful, quite astute and can morph proverbs into jokes. I had not heard anyone misinterpret the well-known proverb from Benjamin Franklin's *Poor Richard's Almanac*, and it was an amusing teaching opportunity.

Consider the much-republished list (found on the Internet) of the first half of well-known proverbs with endings supposedly completed by first graders. Some examples are deemed jokes and fakes due to the advanced answers that seem unreasonable for first graders. The name of the first grade teacher is untraceable due to either ignorance of or failure to honor copyright law or was never given. The list has been copied and republished so many times, that unless the author comes forth, he/she will never be known. Many more teachers since have given the same lesson with delightful results. Knowing the original second half of the proverbs is not necessary to appreciate the humor.

Rich Vocabulary

Misunderstanding is common to all with no exceptions. Some is from processing information literally like children. Truman's oldest son told me that when he was young, he wondered about Psalm 23:1: "The Lord is my Shepherd; I shall not want" (KJV), thinking, "Why don't I want Him?" The King James English is often beautiful and poetic, but passages like this must be explained or updated to modern English for smaller children who are so very literal and for readers unacquainted with Old English. You may have heard the story about a small boy asking, after hearing the lyrics to *Silent Night,* "Who's Round John Virgin?"

The decline of rich vocabulary limits accurate communication and is noticeable in my lifetime. Several examples of changed and "flipped" meanings are found in the Old English language of the King James Bible published over 400 years ago. Modern flipped examples are *bad* can mean *good*, and *hot* and *cool* are also adjustable according to the subject, generation and audience. The use of the popular and annoying word *whatever* is a response to any situation in lieu of dealing with it. Much common speech has become more crude and heard way too frequently, such as formerly taboo and scatological public expression, emphatically corrected in children with soap applied to the mouth. Some vocabulary is like a foreign language if you are not a member of the *hood*.

Controlling the Tongue

The Holy Spirit will help in thinking before speaking and to express ideas and thoughts accurately. Scripture tells us that if we bridle our tongues, we will be perfect (James 3: 2-10). The Lord does not tell us to aim for something unachievable. Do you recognize your need for help in this area?

Just think of the damaging words scripted on social media sites. Bullying has always existed but has now caught national attention due to its scope and damage. The old adage, "Sticks and stones may break my bones, but words will never hurt me," *is not true*. Words can hurt so deeply that lives have been derailed from truth, and suicide has been the horrific and tragic result for some who are not sure who they are or whether anyone would care if they were gone.

The Art of Hearing

We hear what we want to hear is an empirically proved fact. I have heard my words twisted to mean the exact opposite of what I plainly said. The human mind is astonishing. Expressing ourselves correctly is not always the problem. The hearing is also critical.

All public gatherings have distractions of environment, other people, daydreaming, meditating on "to-do" lists or anxiety over personal situations. I actually observed a church elder's wife (!) writing her grocery list during a sermon. Some inattention has to do with diagnosed ADD and ADHD victims. Successful teachers have adjusted methods increasingly from the hearing mode by adding the visual and kinetic (movement) modes, because many more children and adults learn first visually or with movement. This may be due to the whole realm of heavy visual stimulation—decades of movies, TV, video games, advanced technology and possibly sugar overload. Different learning styles have always manifested in any culture, and master teachers have intuitively and creatively addressed them. The recognition that rigid teaching methods have repeatedly resulted in dropouts and graduating children who cannot read or compute has impacted teacher preparation courses. All methods so far have failed to totally correct the problem.

Counteractions

In spite of faulty hearing, that may still be the most important mode. Diverse methods can support the hearing process for accurate, solid and lasting instruction. Weaving fine arts into core curricula and as extra-curricular activities noticeably enhances the entire learning process by melding the hearing, visual, and kinetic modes. Research the compiled SAT test results, which clearly show higher scores for students who have studied the fine arts.[1]

How can misunderstandings be corrected? First, do not assume the listener has heard correctly. A standard classroom technique is to ask for a repeat or an accurate rewording from the listener but

---

1. K. Vaughn & E. Winner. "SAT Scores of Students Who Study the Arts: What We Can \and Cannot Conclude about the Association." *Journal of Aesthetic Education.* (2000) Vol. 3/4. 77-89.

is quite awkward outside the classroom. However, we can repeat or restate what we said. Inattention and/or limited knowledge spawn misunderstandings, and differences of opinions not clearly stated can increase to arguments and deep strife. For multiple reasons, too many students have dropped out of school, insert expletives from inadequate vocabularies, lack work ethics and skills and most importantly, lack critical discernment between truth and lies.

"Charged" Communication

How can correct understanding be verified in a highly emotional conversation? Some very obvious and wisest strategies are thinking before speaking (refraining from sounding off) and choosing specific words thoughtfully and carefully. Self-control must be practiced to always be the first response. An important proverb teaches, "a soft answer turns away wrath, but a harsh word stirs up anger (Proverbs 15:1)." Courtesy is always in vogue.

One of my favorite tongue-in-cheek statements is, "How do I know what I think till I hear what I have to say?" This statement means speaking can clarify issues that have remained in the mind in an unformed state. It is also an amusing reminder that what we speak is what we believe. Lack of thinking before speaking can be a revelation or embarrassing.

Memory Bank Deposits

The current reading levels for printed media are estimated to be sixth through eighth grades—a worrisome fact. To build a memory bank full of good word choices, purposely work at increasing vocabulary. Reading material requiring a dictionary or thesaurus has the potential to accelerate learning with more subject matter and new words for accurate communication. Associating with educated people can help increase vocabulary, because mere conversation with new words can infer the definitions from the context and tone.

Active, Not Passive

We can be careful in speaking and in correcting what we say, but what about the listener? Hearing involves a decision on the part of the hearer to listen or ignore, accept or reject what has been spoken.

We cannot do much about how someone else hears except pray we will be accurate, and they will hear correctly.

Jesus emphasized the importance of hearing several times in His teachings. He said, "He who has an ear, let him hear what the Spirit says to the churches" (Revelation chapters 2 and 3), repeating it seven times in a single weighty message to the representative churches about their doctrine and practices.

The extensive listing of the verb *to hear* and all its grammatical forms in Bible concordances and dictionaries demonstrates its magnitude. The Greek word *akouo* means to *hear and understand.*[2] Stereo hearing appendages on each side of our heads obviously do not guarantee correct hearing. Therefore, the physical hearing is not the crux of the issue in most cases, so megaphones are unnecessary. If there is no need for hearing aids, then the hearing problem goes deeper than our physical ears.

The Deeper Issue

Why do people misunderstand something that seems obvious? Our son interpreted the common proverb literally because he had limited information at his age to make the health connection to apples. Selective hearing only reaffirms the fact that the soul will filter input according to knowledge, preferences, attitudes and prejudices and operates under the following conditions:

— When we already believe or suspect something negative about a speaker, we will most likely reject or misunderstand anything the speaker says.

— When we believe positive things about a speaker, we are more disposed to accept what is said.

— When we do not have a teachable soul or a love for truth, we will not receive new information and will be vulnerable to being deceived (2 Thessalonians 2: 10-11).

— If misunderstandings have accumulated without resolution, we will need assistance to recognize truth.

---

2. Taken from: *The New Strong's Complete Dictionary of Bible Words* ©.by James Strong ©. Used by permission of Thomas Nelson.

Hearing and speaking are truly spiritual issues. Both require the Lord's guidance, intervention and correction. What and how we hear and speak are gravely important. A critical issue: "So then *faith* comes by hearing, and hearing by the *word of God* (Romans 10:17, emphasis added)."

Hearing God

I must constantly ask the Lord to help me hear Him clearly. He speaks through His Word, His creation and other people to our spirits through His still small voice (2 Corinthians 5:10-11; 1 Kings 19:11-12). Misunderstanding and confusion about God"s Word is the human default setting, either because we have not heard the truth about God, practiced listening to Him or we are reluctant to give up control. Our growing years trains us to make decisions on incomplete information, limited understanding and sometimes faulty advice from others. Scripture admonishes *not* to rely on human understanding (Proverbs 3:5-8). Instituting the Lord's plan for us requires getting His directions for every detail and is infinitely more certain than human counsel. This is not hard—just ask Him for help—then listen. He wants us to hear Him and He wants to hear from us. He speaks primarily through His Word.

His purpose for creating us was for fellowship with Him. He is a very nice Person! He can be our Best Friend—our Ultimate Friend. Removing ourselves from the thrones of our hearts allows Him to take His proper place as King over our individual kingdoms.When He establishes His Kingdom in us, our spiritual ears and eyes will be opened to hear and understand accurately.

Moral Of The Story
— *Practical lesson:* Read voraciously with a dictionary or thesaurus handy to expand vocabulary.
— *Spiritual lesson:* Pray for grace from God to hear Him and others accurately and to speak accurately.

What else might be learned from this anecdote/devotional?

Language

Audible or written, I'm revelation.
The was, is and will be I make known.
Words and letters a foundation
For knowledge or specific tone.
Height or depth of communication,
A precious gift to us alone,
Becomes a welcome celebration
Or expresses the deepest groan.

A consonant or vowel, a sound, a word
Resonates consciousness of being.
Whether significant, profound or even absurd,
Words make audible the act of seeing.
Understanding gives birth to inner vision,
Freshness, illumination, creativity,
Expressed uniquely in personal decision
With emphasis on clarity.

Diane Shields Spears ©

Wordsmith

I want to be a wordsmith,
One who chooses words with
Cleverness and politeness,
Excellence and eruditeness.
A silver-tongued individual,
One able to debate and duel
With accuracy and precision
While accomplishing my mission.

Wordsmiths invent appellations
To express specific designations.
Fun with words my lofty goal,
Letting impressive utterance roll
Off my tongue with joy and ease,
Vocabulary to tickle and tease.
Delighting hearers with a novel word,
Even risking being absurd.

English has its limitations—
Words with several definitions.
Foreign tongues seem more efficient
Providing sentences more proficient
With verbs and adjectives showing gender.
In forming sentences they render
More exactness without sweat;
Therefore, I must be a wordsmith-ette.

Diane Shields Spears ©

•••18•••

Albrecht's Brush

● ●

Life comes in three's.

● ●

Hi. I have the distinction and honor of being the favorite brush of the famous artist, Albrecht Durér, who made me for his detail work. I have three major parts: the handle, the ferule and the group of brush hairs. My handle is imported mahogany, the finest and hardest wood available, that Albrecht carefully shaped and sanded satin-smooth to hold me comfortably. My ferule is of polished tin, and my brush hairs are the finest sable, trimmed to the precise shape for his use. He took great care, expense and much time to make me correctly.

I was designed for long life but I will not last forever. The shape of my hairs will eventually change and wear down with use. Albrecht is careful with me though, because, first, I am valuable to him and second, because I am able to place my brush hairs in exactly the right places. He knows what to expect from me. He gently and thoroughly cleans me after each use and does not allow me to soak in solvent that would ruin me.

I am so pleased to be a tool in the hand of such a great master artist. I would puff up with pride, but I fear I would change shape by puffing and then I would not be as useful to him. Besides, I cannot take any credit for what I am, since I did not make myself.

Signed: Albrecht's Favorite.

● ●

Made with a Purpose

Just as the artist's brush was carefully and skillfully made for a specific purpose, so are we. We are not clones. Even identical twins are not 100 percent identical in their DNA or personalities. Our basic common structure is distinct and specially designed with great attention to detail, like a carefully woven tapestry of specific colors and patterns unlike anyone else (Psalm 139:1-18). However, in this fallen world with overwhelming toxins, accidents can happen. Remember, Satan is the destroyer, does not play fair and will try to use any DNA abnormalities and damage in the womb to his advantage and to thwart God's purpose. God will always bring good out of destruction with submission to Him.

In addition to being unique individuals is also a unique purpose for existence here on Earth and for eternity (Jeremiah 29:11-13; Ephesians 2: 10-11). Believe it! Scripture has clues to your destiny and is the bread, water and all the nutrients needed for spiritual and physical health with direction for victorious existence! Your value to God and your specially created purpose for life are like gold that must be mined and purified through the Word. Be a prospector for this gold.

A Good Conscience

Have you ever heard someone say, "There's good in all of us"? That statement must be qualified to: conscience is the *potential* for good. Obviously, not everyone follows a good conscience and everyone has choices of good/better/best or bad/worse/horrible. A seared conscience—one that appears to be nonexistent—is the result of repeatedly ignoring its promptings for correction. The conscience becomes rigid like iron rendering it non-functional (1 Timothy 4:2). Therefore, the penchant for evil latent in all people—even for those considered the best of humanity—should be acknowledged.

For example, babies may not yet know right from wrong and are considered innocent. Nevertheless, without exception they behave selfishly by nature and must be corrected or grow up to be walking disasters. Correction opens understanding to wise choices constantly necessary to be a winner in life. Your children will love you more for correcting them. Likewise, correction from our loving God should make us love Him more, because it is *proof* we are His children (Hebrews 12:5).

The Spiritual Irritant

The Ten Commandments (called The Law of Moses and the Law of

God) is to prompt self-inspection and repentance. The rub is the uncomfortable stirring of guilt feelings produced by them in our consciences. These ten "rules" are certainly a necessary guide for expected behavior *but cannot change the heart*—that disposition of humanity for selfishness, greed, hatred, jealousy and more. All the Law does is reveal how faulty we are—it condemns (Galatians 3:24). The Ten Commandments also do not make individuals and societies play nice at all times.

The Old Testament Israelites had to perform elaborate rituals to be acceptable to God and to be temporarily forgiven—or die. The penalty for breaking the Law was (and still is) death (Romans 6:23). Death is first a spiritual condition that eventually becomes physical.

Fashioned in Three's

All animate and inanimate materials are specially designed for earthly physical systems (2 Corinthians 5:1-2). Just as a brush has three main components (handle, ferrule, and group of brush hairs), so are we created in "three's." Each human earth suit has DNA common to all but with unique individual variations. Are we more than our bodies? Recall the "Dust" anecdote. Most people recognize there is more to us than the physical even if we have not heard or spent time thinking about it. We are more than mud.

The second component is the inner being having the same basic composition for all humanity, but at the same time is also unique for each individual. It is unseen with our eyes but is discerned through actions, attitudes and words. We call this uniqueness the soul or heart, but not the physical heart (Ephesians 3:16; Matthew 5:8, 15, 19; Romans 10:10). The soul also is three parts: mind (intellect), will (freedom of choice) and emotions. Each of these three operates in and affects the physical body that manifest in unique personalities.

The third and most important part is the spirit. In certain biblical contexts, the spirit is included in the phrase inner being along with the soul/heart. The spirit is the part of human life that communes with the Creator. The spirit was created to hear from God and then instruct the soul/heart to control the body. Instead, in this fallen world, the strongest influences and problems for people are the soul and the body dictating to the spirit. Understanding which part of our three-part being is in control cannot be accurately discerned without God's help (Hebrews 4:12).

Mid-term Exam

23 Search me, O God, and know my heart; try me, and know my anxieties;
24 And see if there is any wicked way in me, and lead me in the way everlasting (Psalm 139: 23-24).

The purpose of asking the Lord to examine us is not because He is ignorant of our faults. He knows us inside and out and better than we know ourselves. We can grieve Him, but it is impossible to shock Him. The issue is our learning what is really inside us. If we truly want a close relationship with the Lord, we should be willing to let Him cast the searchlight on our innermost parts. Most of us have dark areas hidden from our view through self-deception, or just not dealing with issues. The goal is maturity in the Lord through the sanctification (separation from sin and dedication to God) process. If we want to maintain communication with the Lord, we must deal with dark areas when He reveals them to us. How do we deal with them? We repent, ask for forgiveness and ask the Lord to help us please Him.

Futility of Religion

A religion is simply a belief system that guides a person. Therefore, even atheism, philosophies and political "-isms" are religions. All religions of the world (except Christianity) have one major common philosophy: we must do the searching for God and impress Him with good works that outweigh the bad. However, earning brownie points with God through self-effort is impossible. Christianity properly understood stands on a different foundation:

— It recognizes that no human descendant of Adam can be good enough to reach God's holiness standard through self-effort —i.e. works/deeds (Romans 3:10).
— We are in need of a Divine Substitute who obeyed the Holy Spirit perfectly for us to take the judgment we deserve.

— Jesus *searches* for us! This is a critical difference between Christianity and all other belief systems. He loved us way before we loved Him (Romans 5:8; 1 John 4:10, 19). He desires a relationship with us even more than we desire it with Him. He seeks us, and then gives us grace and faith necessary to come to Him (Ephesians 2:4-9). That's love!

Spiritually Disabled

Becoming cerebral about how we tick can be confusing because human understanding is limited and faulty. Everyone—all human beings—have a default spiritual learning disability and need to be educated in God's Word. This disability is not physical, mental or emotional. Repeat—it is spiritual. To function as designed, the spirit should have access to and respond to more information than what is sensed only in the soul or body. For example, emotions are unreliable—we can be shaken by fear when there is nothing to fear.

Competing Frequencies

Many voices clamor to be heard through electromagnetic spectrum frequencies whether physically or spiritually heard. These visual and audio waves are remarkable. Stories circulate about short wave radios picking up decades old broadcasts! Our words are still out there in the ether! They are recorded in heaven and God will judge us according to every word we speak (Matthew 12:36). Will you now think about that before sounding off?

Caution! Not all voices speak truth, so be careful about tuning in to any old frequency out there. Tuning into the Lord's frequency will cause gradual changes that permit our God-designed purpose to become a reality. Constant connection to His frequency requires that we be born again, a phrase that has been mishandled by many who apply it to anything new.

Tuning into God's frequency will be the communion experience with Him that your heart has been longing for since your physical birth on this orb. Perhaps you were just not aware of it until now.

Renewal

What will change us from the inside out to be pleasing to the Lord?

The Ten Commandments have power to convict but no power to transform. We can earnestly desire to be perfect by obeying all the Commandments, but cannot attain it under our own steam. Good news! The Lord Jesus already did it for us! It took God Himself to solve our fatal spiritual heart condition. True Christianity is not just a religion but is a relationship with a Person—the Lord Jesus Christ, the Messiah. Everything about this heart transformation is based on Him, not just on a set of ideals to live by. We learn that living solely by ideals simply reveals how really powerless and empty we are.

An Alert

You were previously warned you might encounter information and ideas that contradict your background education or personal beliefs. If you struggle with the following information, I urge you to keep your opinions at bay until you have thoughtfully and honestly read to the end. If you still disagree, then opposing ideas will have at least challenged you, and you will know why you accept some ideas and reject others. Applying critical thought processes in choosing between different or opposing concepts is true education, not just being told by so-called authorities and self-appointed experts what to think and believe. Be intellectually honest to be able to stand for your opinions and beliefs and not be swayed by public opinion.

The Battle Against Individuality

Many human philosophies, some religions and the many political "-isms" pressure society toward uniformity for so-called utopian ideals that eventually and effectively suppress the uniqueness of individuals through governmental control. Reminder: humanism is a dead end that exalts self—self-sufficiency and self-confidence. These selfish ideologies devalue others through usury on a grand scale. Denial of God-given freedoms is the clue to recognizing dysfunctional systems.

When we examine social and political philosophies, psychology, humanism, all other "-isms" and *evolution* (all of which bear "bad fruit"), we expose the deep roots of atheism. Verified scientific information shows evolution is an illogical humanistic philosophy and is therefore, one of the strongest branches of atheism.

If you know only about evolution, the previous paragraph might have tempted you to throw down this book in prejudgment of the conclusions. The tree of evolution actually bears rotten fruit by reducing us all to cosmic accidents and mere animals, totally eradicating any purpose for existence. Evolution and all major religions and philosophies of the world, except Christianity, are only mental exercises, promoting ideals with sets of rules and precepts to control behavior, achieve dreams, and change people for the better. However, *just like the Ten Commandments,* they have no power for real heart transformation to change the undesirable inner motivations causing all the problems for the soul and societies.

The Lord tells us He is a jealous God (Deuteronomy 4:24; Exodus 20:5, and more). Comparing scriptures leads to the conclusion that the Lord's utmost jealousy is that of His being the Creator. The doctrine of evolution is contrary to Scripture in two major ways. God emphatically states that He *spoke* the creation into existence, and using evolution as His creating method requires death to the unfit. Scripture states plainly that death is God's enemy and will be the last enemy to be destroyed (1 Corinthians 15:26). God is *life*. More information will be in the sequel to this book.

Spiritual Maintenance

The term *born again* is specific and refers to only one thing—reconnecting human spirits to God the Father by regeneration through the Lord Jesus, the Christ, the Messiah. Jesus explained this carefully to Nicodemus, an advanced teacher of the Law in a high position of authority and who should have already understood the need for regeneration (John 3:1-17). Nicodemus believed and helped bury the body of Jesus after the crucifixion.

How do we maintain the connection with God's frequency once we have become born-again? Prayer, praise, worship and reading God's Word are essential—all taking time. Memorizing scriptures is exceedingly valuable, making deposits to our memory banks for something to recall when needed. If you also memorize the scripture "address"—great! However, memorization without heart involvement could produce only a mental relationship with the Lord. Again, speaking the Word of God audibly to hear our own voices augments and embeds Scripture in our souls and spirits. Attitudes and behavior gradually change to become who and what God wants us to be and do. The process is daily, not instantly.

The Lord Jesus not only taught the ideals of morality, He lived them for us as the Anointed One. The Hebrew *Messiah* and Greek *Christ* are synonymous for *anointing*, meaning *authorized for service*. Only Jesus bears the titles Christ/Messiah because He fulfilled God's plans to destroy Satan's power over human beings. Jesus' disciples (born-again believers) receive anointing to spread the Gospel of Jesus.

People can be saved from hell's permanent destruction only because Jesus fulfilled all the Law's requirements for us as our substitute. He took the all the punishment at the Cross of Calvary for all humans and is the only One qualified because of His sinlessness.

Imagine the suffering our Lord endured when He took upon Himself all the punishment for every person who ever lived or will live on this planet! Therefore, it is a "done deal." Everyone's sin is covered, but that gift *must be received for application to individuals.* Hearing a medical report of a crucifixion is unforgettable and boggles the mind. That describes only the physical suffering. Jesus also, for the first time at the Cross, endured temporary and agonizing separation from the Father. He took our place in judgment and rose victoriously from death to give us eternal life in Him.

We have been created individually and uniquely. An exact replica of you will never be found (past, present, or future). Like the proverbial snowflake, God's infinite ability to create makes you a VIP in His sight.

Moral Of The Story
— *Practical lesson:* Self-directed remakes do not produce eternal results.
— *Spiritual lesson:* You did not create you. Let the Matchless Creator guide your remake according to His highest purpose already planned for you.

What other lessons might be contained in this parable?

● ● ● 19 ● ● ●

Cockleburs

● ●

God will not attend our pity parties.

● ●

Inspired by a message at church, a wannabe gardener planted a vegetable garden. The preacher taught about seeds being like big miracles in tiny packages that just grow mysteriously (Mark 26:28). Assured of having God's power on his side, he bypassed research, confident he knew exactly what to do despite his inexperience.

With planting completed, he proudly admired his work. After several days, he spied cottontail rabbits munching on new veggie shoots. In astonishment he shrieked, "Where did you thieves come from? Get outta here! Now! Shoo! Git!" Several cottontail episodes revealed the need for a fence or a scarecrow. Greatly annoyed at this inconvenience, a scarecrow was hastily built with help from his kids but was ineffective.

Not willing to spend more money, he sat on the patio to think, looking around for something useful as a fence. His scrutiny focused on some cocklebur weeds too near the patio, shaming and reminding him of his kids' complaints about the thorns while playing outside and his procrastination of yard cleanup. His eyes widened with a bright idea. He leaped to his feet overjoyed he could solve two problems with one action. He was quite sure the stickers would discourage animal foragers even better than an expensive fence and besides, he mused, it would be easier. This foolish gardener began carefully transplanting the thorny cockleburs to the perimeter of the garden for a fence.

Fortunately, rains came at opportune times, because he was counting on not wasting time watering. Everything flourished in spite of his neglect, including the cockleburs. Noticing the maturing veggies, he was quite dismayed to also discover the cockleburs had not kept their assigned place and had infiltrated the veggie rows, prospering twice as fast as the veggies. He began weeding only to be repeatedly poked through his socks and gloves. He resisted the temptation to cuss, biting his tongue with great effort, only because his kids were outside playing. At full harvest time, he had lovely veggies and a still wildly abundant, healthy and stubborn crop of cockleburs.

He now had the hard work of digging up the weeds by the roots and burning them before the rest dropped their seeds. This was sweaty, laborious and frustratingly slow and with advancing anger. A feeble attempt at muffling a roar and beating the ground with the shovel a few times sent his wide-eyed kids instantly into the house. Pacing the kitchen, he fumed to his wife, putting her in a bad mood and then scattered the kids and dog by yelling at them to scram. The veggies were maturing past their prime, and many of the cockleburs had already seeded for next year. Anger began morphing into depression.

Moping and complaining in self-pity, the gardener then cried out to the Lord for help, hoping the Lord would work a miracle and make the cockleburs vanish.

The Lord answered with, "You didn't ask me for wisdom, or I would have provided for a fence, shown you how to build it and how to care for your crops every day, not just when you were ready for the harvest. You would have truly enjoyed this project. Also read for yourself Mark 4:26-28 about seeds, and I'll show you its real interpretation."

The sorry gardener, still hopeful the Lord would undo the stickers decision with a miracle, responded with, "Oh, Lord, please forgive me!"

The Lord answered, "I forgive you and I still love you, but you must ask your family and your dog for forgiveness too. Laziness got you into this predicament, so you now must reap what you sowed (Galatians 6:7). You have some hard work to do, so get busy. Next time, ask Me first."

• •

Cockleburs (grass, sand burs) describe several weeds with spiny, prickly heads needing no encouragement to take over land. The slightest brush against the developed dry burs dislodges them from the stems, thereby clinging to clothes and animal hair and poking skin. The foolish gardener's pitiful judgment and lack of common wisdom is obvious. He misinterpreted a statement made at church about seeds sprouting like big miracles from miniature packages without discerning the Scripture's intent and context. Mark 4:26-28 does not state or imply gardens need no care. The meaning: God created seeds to grow and causes the earth to produce by its own inherent composition. The scripture actually alludes to the mystery of life, still an enigma to science and remains in God's omniscience.

Garden and Weed Metaphors
A garden is an appropriate symbol for human life, and weeds are apt metaphors for anything that chokes proper living (2 Corinthians 10:3-5).

Spiritual weeds are enemies, and ignoring warnings from the conscience allows sneaky weeds to infiltrate our gardens, whether intentionally or unintentionally, because we are imperfect. Efforts to eradicate the roots often meet a wall of helplessness and defeat when self is in charge, revealing the necessity for God's help for permanent, eternal results. He will expose the roots-causes of our weed crops to set in motion repentance on our part and forgiveness and deliverance on His part. Let Him show you His goodness.

True Nature of Weeds
Truman is victorious over cockleburs on our property due mainly to *diligent weed warfare.* Likewise, a willingness to allow the Lord's searchlight to examine the contents of our souls will expose weeds and their roots for removal. Spiritual warfare requires first to recognize unrighteous issues-weeds as what they really are—*sin.*

Sin is a word people tend to avoid, rationalizing and softening the sting by labeling it mistakes, wrong turns, bad choices, wrong thinking and such. *Merriam-Webster's Collegiate® Dictionary,* offers thirty-four synonyms and vernacular substitutions for the tiny, but powerful word *sin*[1] that infers judgment.

---

1. "By permission. From *Merriam-Webster's Collegiate® Dictionary, 11th Edition* ©2015 by Merriam-Webster, Inc. (www.Merriam-Webster.com)."

Spiritual Virus

The simplest and perhaps the most accurate definition of sin is a literal translation from the Greek: *to miss the mark*.[2] The mark to aim for is God's nature—flawlessness, perfection, righteousness and holiness. The strongest word in Scripture for sin is *iniquity*[3] from the Hebrew, and is defined as "perverseness, to be bent or crooked and the tendency or penchant to do wrong." Iniquity is "unequal-ness" to God's holiness, preventing everyone from hitting that mark of perfection and holiness through self-effort. Adam's rebellion perverted the inherent nature of humanity from purity to sinfulness. *Just like computer malware, iniquity infected, deadened and reprogrammed the souls of Adam and Eve to be attracted to sin.*

Since we are all descendants of Adam, our inherited "fallen-from original-grace" nature causes us to commit personal sin and makes us unworthy to enter into God's presence. Herein is a clue to the struggles between obedience and disobedience for all who give themselves to the Lord. Good news! God has *permanently reversed* this hopeless dilemma! The solution is available to all!

Spiritual Default

If you have ever struggled to be free of something you know is not right, you realize you are stuck with a *spiritual-moral handicap*. In all people, iniquity is a blemished, defective state, a default spiritual disability. It misses the mark of perfection and prevents and/ or interferes with proper connection to God. We are born on this Earth physically alive but spiritually inert ("dead") and unable to fellowship with Him. Sin finds its Petri dish in personality-soul fault lines, and is like radio static obstructing transmission and reception for a connection to the Lord. An uninterrupted connection to God's frequency is desired but the sin and iniquity static must be resolved.

Weed Crops

Weed crops can originate from conscious or subconscious sinful reactions-responses-attitudes to any negative circumstance whether

---

2.   Taken from: *The New Strong's Complete Dictionary of Bible Words*.by James Strong ©. Used by permission of Thomas Nelson.
3.   Ibid.

from poor personal choices or outside forces. Sin is easily seen if an action produces some kind of destruction and/or confusion (John 10:10). The real decisive factor—*whatever is not of faith in God is sin* (Romans 14:23; 2 Corinthians 5:7). Ouch!

The gardener's many mistakes spawned negative reactions and only added to his difficulties. Planting cockleburs was not gross sin but was outrageously foolish and certainly led to sin. *Sin can hide and incubate in poor choices.* Venting his frustration and anger on his family and dog eventually spiraled down to self-pity and depression. Not accepting deserved blame was and always is sinful. Situations tend to go awry when the Lord is not consulted for direction and wisdom.

Self-Deception
Humanity's breeding ground for weeds are deception and ignorance of the inherited default condition of original sin. Deception's main goal is to disable the ability to recognize truth, to spread confusion about Who God really is and to maintain and widen the relationship gap between God and His creation. Ignorance is a choice.

Do you think you are a good person? Many respond with, "Yeah, I think I'm a good person. I may not be perfect, but I do more good than bad." Mark 10:18 records words of the Lord Jesus: ". . . No one is good but One, that is, God." Jesus was opening his follower's understanding to realize he was comparing himself with other people and God. Like the unrighteous Pharisee, self-justification thanks God for being better than the sinner next door and is an abominable attitude in God's opinion. Not enough people recognize the truth of the following anonymously inspired quotation: "God does not grade on the curve. He grades on the Cross." His standard is 100 percent holy credit—or none.

Deadly Mistakes
Moral mistakes are deadly—eternally deadly (Galatians 6:7). God cannot allow sin in His presence, but not because He is angry with us. On the contrary, He loves us so much that He shields us from the power and purity of His presence that would kill us, because God is a consuming fire (Deuteronomy 4:24; Hebrews 12:29).

God hates the sin because it destroys human beings that He created and loves. He does not want anyone destroyed in the fire of His presence or in hellfire. He wants all to be with Him (1 Timothy 2:3-4) and has instituted the perfect plan to accomplish that goal. Sadly, not everyone will believe and will not reap the benefits. Jesus conquered all sin, so *lives surrendered to Him are counted 100 percent righteous, holy and worthy of His presence*. It works no other way.

The Antidote

True repentance is to change your mind and turn away—a U-turn from previous sin. Our wannabe gardener was sorry, but we could infer he had not yet repented, because he did not recognize his culpability and still wanted the Lord to work a miracle to reverse his foolish cockleburs decision. No repentance acts as a prophecy of future mistakes in other situations through lack of wisdom and correct discernment.

A Major Struggle

Many fear they have committed the unpardonable sin and can never be forgiven. To begin, if you are worried about this, you are not guilty, because the Holy Spirit is working conviction in you. Specific scriptures identify unforgiveable sin—refusal to repent, refusal to forgive others and blasphemy against the Holy Spirit. An abundance of scriptures assure us if we accidentally sin, we will be forgiven when we ask and repent.

Hearts can deceive and unforgiveness can hide in dark corners of the soul. God never asks us to forget an event—it could be our teacher. Instead, sincere forgiveness removes the toxic and *deadly* emotion connected to it. Unforgiveness is more harmful for us than for those who are to be forgiven. The ones we need to forgive often are ignorant of the fact they have offended or hurt us, and they proceed blissfully with their lives while we stew in the poison.

Perhaps the most recited Scripture is the famous Lord's Prayer that includes the request for forgiveness and assurance from God of forgiveness when we forgive others. The two very important verses following the *Amen* of verse thirteen are mostly ignored:

14 "For if you forgive men their trespasses, your heavenly Father will also forgive you.

15 But if you do not forgive men their trespasses, neither will your Father forgive your trespasses (Matthew 6:14-15).

Verse fifteen plainly states that the refusal to forgive others will reap unforgiveness from God *for that issue*. The inability to forgive might or might not alter your eternal destiny for heaven, but it will surely rob you of rewards. Do not gamble with your future. The Lord expects us to forgive—*just like He did.*

Some people and events are very difficult to set aside, but God never requires the impossible. He helps us to truly forgive and to eventually learn from the circumstances.

Practicing Holiness

Is it even possible to practice holiness? The qualified answer is *yes*. Holiness can be practiced, but not in human strength. Humanity's best attempts will not transform the default spiritual disability into holiness. We will always fall short of perfection without God's cleansing through accepting what Jesus already did for us (Romans 3:23). Reminder: good deeds generated by self-effort outweighing bad deeds on a heavenly balance scale will not impress God or earn heavenly citizenship.

Your Perception

How do you see your Heavenly Father? Do you see Him as an angry God? Do you compare Him to an imperfect earthly father? Do you see Him as all love (which He is)—but as a permissive Heavenly Father Who always forgives even if you do not repent? Do you think your intentions to be good will count with Him? How you perceive Him will strongly influence your decisions.

Alert: Actions can be deadly and can lead to premature physical death, but might or might not disqualify you from heaven. Anyone who knows the Lord, but purposely yields to temptation with full knowledge of consequences (Hebrews 6:4-6) definitely gambles with God's grace. Your rewards and possibly your entrance into heaven would be affected by consicously hanging onto known sin, even if you have already given your life to the Lord. All sin will be judged eventually because He will not tolerate sin in His presence. Nothing is hidden from Him, so let Him search your heart now.

Living for the Lord should be taken seriously. The Lord is not pleased with half-heartedness or a get-out-of-hell-free decision without a true relationship with Him. Like a marriage contract—be loving and faithful until death. Jesus hit the mark of perfection, and when we are born again, His life and perfection become ours. The greatest moral mistake with eternal negative consequences is to disrespect what God has already given freely. Simple—really.

Moral Of The Story
— *Practical lesson:* Unwise choices are from Satan's rotten garden. Learn what brings wisdom.
— *Spiritual lesson:* God can forgive you for planting sin, but you must do the hard work of weeding your heart with the sharp arrows of the Word of God.

What other lessons are embedded in this chapter?

. . . .
Scar
. . . .

I didn't dare dream I could be the one
To bear this dreadful, historical scar.
To lift up to You Your Only Son,
And help put an end to this deadly war.

Oh, Lord, what an honor! But yet—a small fear—
To be pierced with Your nails while holding You high,
To be stained with Your blood—feel the wound of the spear,
Know the shame of man's sin—watch Your followers cry.

I would take all Your pain if only I could,
But all I can do is just hold You up.
I'll be part of Your Plan by just being wood,
And help You to drink the dregs of the Cup.

We've all been groaning, travailing in pain,
Awaiting Your coming and Your Salvation;
This curse on the Earth has made us insane,
And we've suffered so with Man's humiliation.

And now it's in sight—we've waited for ages:
For fulfillment of Your Perfect Plan,
To blot out the curse while our enemy rages,
Restoring creation by Your purchase of Man.

Diane Shields Spears ©

20

Coyote and Roadrunner

Simple creatures—simple lessons.

Coyote's name is a pun.
To watch him is so much fun.
His wily inventions
Just prove his intentions
To capture his lunch on the run.
Roadrunner is smarter than Wile E.
His speed is amazing while he,
Avoiding all traps,
Gives Wile E. mishaps,
And escapes ol' Coyote with glee.
Will Wile E. ever give up?
All his strategies pile up or blow up.
Roadrunner zooms away;
We shout hip-hip-hooray.
But Coyote warms up for a shakeup.

Diane Shields Spears ©

A famous animated cartoon repeating the same theme in each episode features a roadrunner with whirling jet speed feet and Wile E. Coyote. The coyote continually sets clever and elaborate physical traps but is always thwarted, and the roadrunner always manages to narrowly escape being the coyote's dinner. Wile E. is an appropriate metaphor for the wiles of our adversary, the Devil (Satan), who sets spiritual traps for all people, seeming to never be discouraged, run out of methods or tire of using his successful ones.

First Peter 5:8 states the Devil lurks as a roaring lion seeking anyone he might devour. He is not a real lion—he is only like one—an imitation, an imposter, loud and scary. However, he is dangerous for those without God-given spiritual weapons or who deny God's existence. Human strength and intellect are no match for him. At this time, Satan has limited authority to work in the physical realm but his main weapons are against human minds, wills and emotions.

Intellectual Fog and Mud

A real kingdom of darkness and evil is serious about our destruction. Doubters of this fact will wallow in a murky world of deception and rationalization about why bad stuff happens to "good" people. Deception spreads a mental fog—the real insanity of the world—erases standards of behavior and raises doubts about any purpose for life. "God is not the author of confusion" (1 Corinthians 14:33). Satan muddies the waters to scramble our thinking and to block us from truth.

Satan is a created angel and enjoyed an exalted place in God's kingdom—like Michael the archangel (one of the good guys), but Satan defected. Recognizing Satan is a real being with real powers, is 100 percent evil and is in total opposition to the more powerful God, will prepare us believers to be winners. Satan is God's main opposition, *but he is not God's equal.* No entity is greater than *Jehovah—Elohim* (God the Father, God the Son Jesus, and God the Holy Spirit). However, Satan and his hoard are more powerful than humans who are yet without God's protection. Born-again believers have divine protection and authority over the enemy's wiles, but it must be exercised properly according to God's Word to be effective.

The Enemy's Modus Operandi (M.O.)

Satan's tactics against humanity are not new:

— deception—his starting point and primary strategy. If he is
   successful, he will have stolen our joy, which makes us
   vulnerable to all the following list:
— fear, confusion,
— rebellion,
— sickness, disease, weakness of the flesh,
— accidents, destruction,
— lack, poverty,
— sins of the soul and body (called "flesh" in Scripture),
— death.

Satan's success with deception allows him to afflict and inflict many troubles. He is an expert deceiver, the father of lies and the author of all sin (John 8:44). He conducts his business on everyone using four main *whopping lies* that:

— he doesn't exist,
— evil is unreal—a state of mind,
— he is simply a force,
— he is just as powerful as God,
— God cannot be trusted.

Wartime Vulnerabilities

Every human being is involved in a life-or-death spiritual battle with a real evil personality-entity-spirit, whether or not it is known, understood or believed. Especially stay alert and be prepared to resist Satan and his cohorts—our dedicated enemies, who seek to devour anyone with spiritual weakness in any area. *Satan does not play fair.* He keeps us in his sights and will use any means to destroy us that *we make available* to him. He does not give up trying to ruin us, so we must never give up our warfare against him either.

All humanity is vulnerable from imperfections and weaknesses. Some could be:

— lack of diligence in prayer,
— ignorance of the goodness of God,
— ignorance about Satan's strategies,
— neglecting reading and studying the Word of God,
— too busy with unimportant or even important stuff,
— disobedience to the Holy Spirit's leading,
— un-confessed sin.

Vulnerabilities also stem from incomplete understanding of truth. The road to advanced understanding is life-long, but God's Word contains clearly stated strategies for the stressful here and now to erect defenses against the Devil's wiles. The good news: this warfare is not about fighting in our own strength.

The Believer's M.O.

Spiritual warfare is not with flesh and blood but with evil spirits identified as principalities, powers and rulers of darkness of human systems (Ephesians 6:10-18). With the Lord's guidance, this will not be so scary. The Word and the Holy Spirit's power provides spiritual weapons in the name of the Lord Jesus Christ, the Messiah. Defenses against Satan's wiles are simple but *not necessarily easy*:

1. *Knowing the truth:* The truth about God—He is good. He is light. No evil, no darkness, not even a shadow of turning exists in Him (1 John 1:5; James 1:17). Amazing! Just these facts about God are worth a lifetime of study and getting to know Him. Again, easy theology: God is 100 percent good; Satan is 100 percent evil. God is light; Satan is darkness.

   Years ago I read *The Hobbit* and *The Trilogy* by J.R.R. Tolkien. The benefit for me during those troubling years, besides enjoying the make-believe, was the story line that clearly divided good from evil, dispelling the fog of confusion. The tales are really one long allegory that led me to seeking truth. Not considering special effects, the movie versions fade when compared with the superbly written original stories.

2. *God's Word* perfectly addresses every experience category. Our responsibility and joy is to study and find what applies. Try it. Over time, the sharpness of His sword—His Word—will "surgically" remove sinful thinking and habits. Faith in God will grow and peace will linger for longer periods. Repeating God's word is not vain repetition or the current practice of "soaking," which will be addressed in the sequel to this book. The holy angels of God hearken to the voice of God's Word (Psalm 103:20). Speaking the Word aloud in faith *activates God's holy angels* to bring His Word to pass for you. They wait on us to speak.

3. *Speaking the right words:* Our words originate from beliefs, imagination and perhaps motives with self-destructive potential that could or would oppose God and His Word. So, how do we speak the right words, and what exactly are they? God's Words, not ours, are the right words. God's written

Word is holy, because His Son (Jesus, the Word) is holy. Again, the Word is the new "app" that erases iniquity and programs us to be pleasing to God. Direct quotes of God's Word or words in agreement with God's Word will hit and stick to the mark of perfection.

Therefore, instead of speaking what is felt physically or is visible, speak God's Word over negative circumstances. His Word spoken in faith about healing and about Him as the Healer will attack sickness and disease, although it might require sustained repetition until faith kicks in. Troubled emotions will also respond to God's Word about peace and about Him as the Prince of Peace. The two-edged sword of the righteous and perfect Word does a complete job of correctly programming the mind when applied consistently.

4. *Faith (confidence) in God's goodness and love for us:* This faith cannot be fired up in human strength or imagination. God's grace and faith are His first two gifts so that people can even be saved (Ephesians 2:8-9). Faith is the only way to please God (Hebrews 11:6), and He expects us to practice this faith to mature in Him. God gives everyone "the measure of faith"—an equal amount as a starting point (Romans 12:3). Every believer can improve in faith. Faith matures by hearing God's Word, whether through preaching, hearing your inner voice reading or audible voice speaking it (Romans 10:17). Accurate thinking, believing and speaking will make profound victories possible.

5. *Searching your "heart" and repenting often:* The human soul is deceitful and desperately wicked (Jeremiah 17:9). Born again persons are *declared* pure and holy by faith but are not yet whole and perfect. *Sanctification* is a daily process of maturing in the Lord and shedding sinful motives. Scripture confirms God is love (1 John 4:16); God is also just (1 John 1:9). Sin cannot enter His pure and holy presence. For our safety, He has provided that plan to blot out sin and forgive us so we can enjoy His presence without being destroyed.

6. *Worship and praise:* A terrific Bible victory story is about Jehoshaphat (2 Chronicles 20:1-30) a King of Judah, who

had established righteousness in his kingdom by destroying pagan worship sites. A confederation of enemy kings armed to defeat his kingdom. Jehoshaphat was terrified and sought the Lord in public prayer. When he worshiped, fasted and prayed along with his entire kingdom, the Lord gave the unusual battle strategy: send a choir praising and worshiping God ahead of the army. The king obeyed and the enemy fought and killed each other instead of attacking Judah's army! God defeats our enemies but not with human strategies. He has delightful, astonishing, unfathomable and glorious solutions for every spiritual battle that sometimes seem nonsense to the human mind!

7. *Prayer as armor:* All personnel who fight in battle must have armor. God provides the perfect spiritual armor for believers in Christ to be winners over the Devil and his wiles. The armor pieces are compared with the Roman armor (Ephesians 6:10-18) as truth, righteousness, the good news message, salvation, faith and the Word. Listed last is the spiritual weapon of *every kind* of prayer and is the most important piece against the enemy's intrigue.

   Prayer cannot be over-emphasized. No one needs special qualifications to pray. After all, prayer is how believers become believers. No matter how mature a Christian becomes, prayers may still be imperfect, although heart-felt. We can thank the Lord Jesus that His judgment is about heart issues first. He has provided Himself as the Mediator in our prayer efforts as well as in our salvation (1 Timothy 2:5; Hebrews 8:6). This means He receives our puny prayers and perfects them before He presents them to the Father! What a gift! We need not be intimidated about not knowing how to pray!

8. *Continual, whole-hearted submission:* Spending time with the Lord for strength and instruction and letting Him do the hard parts guarantees victory over temptation and emotional roller coasters—easier than trying to correct bad decisions. Consequences of some decisions are irreversible. Postponing or neglecting fellowship with Him,

or disobeying delays maturing and victory. Ask Him for mercy and grace to follow His lead. The Lord Jesus is so much greater than we can ever imagine with our pathetic, finite minds!

On Guard!

Is this good, or is it evil? Does it add-multiply or subtract-divide? These basic questions will augment understanding. Remember: evil is divisive, deceptive and destructive. Dig deeply for the truth, because some glitter is really fool's gold.

Satan is not like Wile E Coyote because the cartoon is funny, and there is nothing humorous about Satan. He is deadly serious about destroying all of God's creation, and we should be more dedicated in preventing him from ruining us and others. However, Satan is like Wile E because, even though he persistently sets traps for us, he will eventually be judged, failing to realize he is a victim of his own deceptions. He is clearly a loser from instigating the crucifixion of our Lord and from misunderstanding God's plan for redemption.

Satan has a dismal future—he knows he is doomed. One day in the future God is going to chain Satan in hell and later fling him into the lake of fire that burns forever, and ever, and ever . . . and with no parole! Satan is raving mad about it, wanting to steal from God as many people as possible to be with him in hell. Be sure you will not be flung in there to keep him company!

The devils believe in God and tremble (James 2:19), but they cannot be saved. Only human beings can receive salvation. The rest of creation is not guilty of sin but suffers from the effects of Adam's rebellion. Only through believing and receiving by faith the substitutionary death of Jesus can we expect a destination of heaven. He is the One to be exalted, Who will in due time exalt us in ways more marvelous than we can imagine (1 Peter 5:6; Matthew 23:12).

Jesus loves you with perfect love and wants to be your Savior and Lord (King, Master, Captain, Director, Pilot, Shepherd, Boss, Friend . . .). However, participation is *not automatic by just being alive or by having the knowledge about salvation*. We must invite Him into our lives and "walk" with Him daily. Ask Him to come into your heart to receive your debt of sin canceled, paid in full.

He has said plainly that all who come to Him fully in faith *and repentance* will be saved (John 6:37).

Inherited Benefits
When you give yourself to God through Jesus Christ, the Messiah, you are immediately adopted into God's family. You will receive authority and power to resist Satan's temptations through God's Word and the Holy Spirit's strength!

Dangerous Assumptions
Many people who are saved experience great joy and expect to be trouble free thereafter. However, being a Christian is not always easy. Salvation places a target on the new born-again soul who must quickly learn Scripture defensive techniques, because Satan intensifies his deceptions to weaken. Jesus warned of trials and tribulations from the majority who wants to self-rule and who criticizes Christians as weak, crazy, stupid, haters and even traitors. Would you be offended with labels like those? The Lord already addressed this: "And blessed is he who is not offended because of Me (Matthew 11:6)." "These things I have spoken to you, that in Me you may have peace. In the world you will have tribulation; but be of good cheer, I have overcome the world (John 16:33)." "Then they will deliver you up to tribulation and kill you, and you will be hated by all nations for My name's sake (Matthew 24:21)."

Hang onto the Lord even if you are threatened with death! It will be worth it all! He tells us in Scripture that we cannot imagine the wonderful things He has in store for us in this life on Earth *and in eternity.* "But as it is written: 'Eye has not seen, nor ear heard, Nor have entered into the heart of man The things which God has prepared for those who love Him (1 Corinthians 2:9).'"

Moral Of The Story
— *Practical lesson:* Embed in your mind the absolute difference between good and evil and how to discern.
— *Spiritual lesson:* Learn to effectively use God's Word against Satan's kingdom of darkness.

What other lessons might be contained in this parable?

• •
Sky Watcher
• •

Barometers, rain gauges, windsocks and such
Add clues to what's been foretold;
But all these fine instruments don't tell me much.
I still peer through windows to watch it unfold.

Thunderheads growing, glowing, impressive,
Blue holes occupying space between,
Gorgeous, gigantic, voluptuous, massive,
Excessive, glorious, overwhelming scene.

High cirrus, quite like hair tufts scattered
In elevated winds capture my attention.
Ice crystals of thin fabric tattered
Appear safe, not worthy of mention.

Condensing stratus darkening and low,
Few moments required for a scene change to sunless.
Deep grays stacking themselves row upon row—
Somehow turning emotions to joyless.

What's left of the blue is overtaken,
Air turning cold, I want a cover;
Watching through glass I find myself shaken,
My attention riveted till the storm is over.

Lightning, thunder, raining in sheets,
Sudden impetus to be sure of protection;
Praying quickly so nothing unseats
My sense of security—my Heavenly Connection.

Clouds and weather—powerful metaphors.
We must not ignore the prophecies or signs:

Inspiring thoughts and images galore,
To strengthen hopes for silver lines.

We see trouble raining on the just and unjust;
No one is exempt from misfortune or pain.
In order to weather the storms we must
Seek the Sure Foundation to stand in the rain.

Diane Shields Spears ©

21

Sky Watcher

··························
You are not required to suffer alone.
··························

Clouds and all kinds of weather can be metaphors *and* paradoxes for life's difficulties, hazards and disasters as well as for protection and blessings. Does every cloud have a "silver lining"? Three origins for the well-known silver lining proverb are attributed to John Milton, Charles Dickens and P.T. Barnum. Each phrased it similarly but in their unique expressions. This popular adage means "something good that can be found in a bad situation, a consoling or hopeful prospect."[1] That encouragement is not easily grasped when troubles look bigger than our abilities.

Hidden Lessons
The silver lining metaphor agrees with Scripture: "And we know that all things work together for good to those who love God, to those who are called according to His purpose (Romans 8:28)." Two qualifiers in this statement are: first, we must love God and second, honor His purpose above personal preferences. We can trust His guidance and ability to make everything right *in His timing*. The Lord's corrections are always good (Hebrews 12:5) even if temporarily uncomfortable or painful.

A Paradox
Although clouds and storms can cause difficulties and concern about the immediate future, they can also bring many blessings. The Old Testament repeatedly refers to rain as a blessing (Isaiah 55:10; Leviticus 26:3-9) and drought as a curse or judgment (Deuteronomy

---

1. "By permission. From *Merriam-Webster's Collegiate® Dictionary, 11th Edition* © *2015* by Merriam-Webster, Inc. (www.Merriam-Webster.com)."

28: 23-24). Think about the areas of the Earth devastated by severe and sustained drought and flooding in the same time frame. Could it be judgment? Flooding and drought are certainly not blessings.

Literal clouds can also be beautiful and inspiring, especially the impressive thunderheads, and can also be reminders of how vast the sky really is. Many poets have written about the sky, clouds and all weather episodes. Dust and water in clouds produce spectacular sunrises and sunsets. "A great cloud of witnesses," surrounds us— redeemed souls and/or angels in heaven, cheering us on to continue in the Lord (Hebrews 12:1). The Lord will come *in the clouds* to call us to be with Him, "the dead in Christ shall rise, and we will be caught up together with them in the clouds (1 Thessalonians 4:17)," popularly known as the *rapture*.

An Awesome Mystery

A mysterious cloud (Exodus 15) hovered over the Israelites' sacred tabernacle, shaded them from the sun and guided them during the day in their journey through the sweltering and challenging wilderness. This awesome cloud was the visible reminder of God's presence and enveloped Moses on his trips to the mountaintop. Moses' face shone so brightly after these experiences in God's presence that he had to wear a veil so people could talk to him.

The cloud became a pillar of fire providing light at night and reassuring their safety in the wilderness. Enemies could see the cloud and pillar of fire and would fear, knowing it was God's supernatural protection over the Israelites. God's cloud and fire also protected the Israelites from getting too close to Him so they would not die in the fire of His presence.

Jesus was enveloped in a cloud on Mt. Transfiguration when Moses and Elijah spoke with Him, witnessed by the Apostles Peter, James and John. This time the cloud did not shield the disciples from God but filtered out all else so they were only aware of Jesus, Moses and Elijah. When the cloud lifted, Jesus "glistened" like Moses' face must have done when he descended Mount Sinai after meeting with God (Mark 9:2-8).

A Fresh Metaphor

I had asked the Lord why I was having some troubles and why some people seem to be more troubled than others. The Lord placed an image in my mind:

Imagine a large yellow poster representing, not the sky, but God's kingdom, His presence and goodness as well as everything anyone needs.

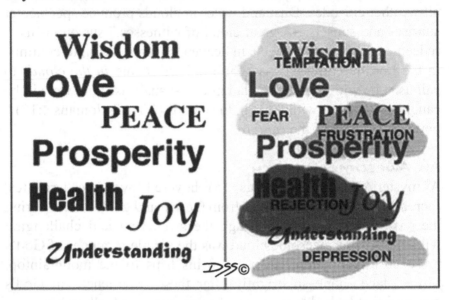

God's kingdom becomes obscured by many different cloud sizes and thicknesses—some overlapping or spaced apart. They represent this "fallen" world's situations and confusion arranged by Satan, the destroyer of life and prince of the power of the air (Ephesians 2:2). The clouds had labels such as trials, sickness, disease, accidents, and other heartaches and destructions. Some *effectively blocked the perception of God's kingdom.*

Deeper Interpretation

Clouds of trouble often depend upon the direction one is taking in life when a particular cloud is encountered. Consider health issues. The body was created to be the Holy Spirit's temple (1 Corinthians 3:16) so, taking care of physical and mental health is a serious responsibility. If good health principles are repeatedly ignored, consciously or subconsciously, the direction chosen could be and most likely would be toward a cloud of sickness or disease. God calls attention to good health information to avert trouble, but the information must be acted upon. Nutrition research has blossomed, so ignorance is unwise and may be without excuse if the information is easily available. God is able and willing to heal, but healing may be delayed by not practicing sensible health principles. Remember, except for God's mercy, whatever is sown will be reaped (Galatians 6:7). Be careful not to take for granted God's grace and mercy by purposely neglecting or violating good health practices for the Holy Spirit's earthly temple.

Changing physical habits to improve health can be difficult and information is often resisted. The Lord may not with sovereignty change a direction we have chosen, because He has given free will to choose personal paths. He wants us to choose health—physical, mental and spiritual. Apart from God's grace, unwise health choices will most likely lead to an unavoidable cloud of sickness -disease. The Lord promised He "will never leave us or forsake us (Hebrews 13:5)." He can and is willing to heal, while guiding us through the cloud (Psalm 103:1-5; Exodus 15:26). He also expects us to  be informed and to use common sense after healing. God is merciful and can override foolish decisions by His grace through faith in Him and His healing Word. The key for always having hope is repentance.

When Troubles Increase

The gradual pile-up of clouds in the third graphic demonstrates confused, unidentifiable issues and times when the weight of trials and difficulties seems unbearable. Even if clouds obscure God's kingdom from consciousness, *it is still where it is supposed to be.*

The clouds visual aid explanation from the Holy Spirit about the source of troubles was very comforting for me, and helps me judge myself. It also provides some answers to why bad things happen to good people and why I have experienced some hardships.

However, this is not the total reason for troubles. More remarks about this subject will be presented in the coming sequel with deeper answers in the chapter, "Can I Control Events in My Life?"

The Lord will rescue when we call out to Him:

> No temptation has overtaken you except such as is common to man; but God is faithful, who will not allow you to be tempted beyond what you are able, but with the temptation will also make the way of escape, that you may be able to bear it (1 Corinthians 10:13).

Temptation refers to both sin and the temptation to give up, because *whatever is without faith is sin* (Hebrews 11:6). In the case of our example of practicing good habits to recover health or reach a desired weight, the temptation to give up can be a continuous battle because restoration is a slow process. Whatever the issue, do not give up. The Lord is always for us, never against us.

> For our light affliction, which is but for a moment, is working for us a far more exceeding and eternal weight of glory (1 Corinthians 4:17).

Darkness

The dark kingdom is real with real power to hinder if we rebel against God, are ignorant or inattentive. During any difficulty, God is able to correct, instruct and guide us by the Holy Spirit Who can expedite the trip through the cloud(s) or rescue victoriously from them. Several scenarios are possible. We could:

— escape trouble clouds by God's infinite grace and mercy,
— acquire wisdom to avoid certain situations for a path between clouds instead of through them,
— walk in the bright light of God's Kingdom for a period of rest

before we encounter another situation,
— praise the Lord *in* (not *necessarily for*) all situations to build faith and be rescued.

The Lord warned that trials and troubles can be relentless, but He promised deliverance if we stay close to Him, the Deliverer. Read again First Corinthians 10:13. The Lord said He would not allow us to suffer or be tempted more than we are able to endure. To give up is a temptation that accompanies all trials or difficulties, and is a major battle of the mind. Will we believe negative circumstances or God's Word of rescue and victory? Letting the Lord guide daily in His paths of righteousness will begin and continue victory and personal maturity to please Him.

Lessons in Everything

Some clouds are not of our choosing but are simply because this world is fallen from its original perfection, and our archenemy aims to steal, kill and destroy (John 10:10). The destructive evil culprits are worldly human thinking, earthly systems in distress and Satan's manipulation of them. Satan will attempt to bring personal disaster as soon as he locates human weakness in any area of the soul. Not all trouble is Satan's fault but he will certainly use anything available. We must assume responsibility for any foolish choices and get help from the Lord to change our thinking and direction. The Lord also knows which cloud lessons we need to continue maturing in Him.

16 Rejoice always,
17 pray without ceasing,
18 *in everything* give thanks; for this is the will of God in Christ Jesus for you. (1 Thessalonians 5:16-18, emphasis added).

When the ordeal is over and *lessons learned*, you will understand why the Lord instructs you to rejoice and be thankful *in and for* everything, because the Lord always works all things around for our good (Romans 8:28).

Being wise means learning something from all situations, positive or negative, with correct interpretations by comparing them with God's Word. Scripture provides an abundance of both positive and negative examples with undeniably strong clues about the interpretations and how they apply to our lives.

An "Any Time" Choice

Repentance is always appropriate and God will forgive when it is sincere, but like the pitiful gardener's cockleburs example, the garden will still require weeding. Sinful actions and responses give Satan opportunity to do his dastardly deeds. Speaking God's Word will eventually counteract unwanted circumstances with lessons learned and redirected thinking patterns.

Thinking and Muttering

Again, hearing the Word of God spoken with our voices and by others builds faith.

Scriptural meditation specifically is thinking on and muttering Scripture. Meditation and speaking the Word repeatedly is like writing it with boldface, italicized, indelible ink on the Holy Spirit's temple walls (the human physical body) and underlining it multiple times. It becomes part of the temple and is embedded in the memory bank of the mind and brain. God's Word is powerful.

The "Apples and Doctors" chapter proposed hearing as the possible ultimate physical and spiritual sense we have for receiving accurate information. Meditating on (audibly repeating Scripture) and memorization are exceedingly valuable in making deposits to our memory banks and building faith in the process. These activities are not vain (useless) repetition. Jesus condemned vain repetition when referring to prescribed prayers that had become routine and mechanical recitations without any mental or heart-felt participation in the process.

Saved From Destruction

Truman tells a story that causes his voice to shake with emotion, sometimes bringing tears. He describes an incident that would be scary for most kids. When he was around ten years old, he, his dad and Leroy, his dad's friend, were enjoying fishing at Medina Lake. Slowly propelled by a two-horsepower motor in a fifteen-foot row boat, they aimed for the south side across the lake and began casting near a cliff. Leroy looked to the north at the sound of thunder.

Approaching like a speeding train, were heavy black clouds, wind and rain. As they turned the boat to head back to their truck, the motor stopped when rain hit exposed wires. The sky darkened, lightning flashed, hail pelted, heavier rain drenched them and the wind and waves became almost unmanageable. Leroy struggled with the oars while Truman's dad bailed water.

The storm was fearsome, probably like what the disciples felt when they had to awaken Jesus for help. That Sea of Galilee storm must have been a humdinger to frighten the passel of experienced commercial fishermen into fearing for their lives. Jesus, asleep in the boat after hours and hours of exhausting ministry, came to their rescue as always by *speaking* to the storm (Mark 4:31-41).

Truman recalls that he was not afraid and was rather enjoying the storm. When asked by his family on arriving home if he had been afraid, he stated he was not scared, because his dad was in the boat with him. He had total confidence his dad could do anything. What a fabulous metaphor of safety about our Heavenly Father watching over us!

The Father's Watch

Our Heavenly Father knows exactly what is happening in and to each person individually at all times. No one but Almighty God could keep track of it all. In the midst of storm-like circumstances, fear does not need to reign. Simply call on Him. The familiar and simple Psalm 23, "The Shepherd's Psalm," comforts with blessings and His assurance that He is with us in the "valley of the shadow of death." If you have not yet memorized this poetic and short Psalm, I encourage you to do so.

Whether or not you had a loving father in your natural family, you can certainly have the Perfect Father now by allowing God to direct your life. He desires to hear from us even when all is OK. We were created for fellowship with Him, and He will take care of us if we let Him. Nothing will ever separate us from Him (Romans 8:35-37)—except ourselves through our God-given freedom of choice. Straying from Him will be disciplined, but staying close to Him will be the the most rewarding experiences of your life.

The Blame Game

Insurance companies, including a significant percentage of the population, declare major natural disasters as "acts of God." This could be true for specific weather incidents, since God has used natural events as discipline in the past. World systems are quite willing to blame God for all the disasters without learning the lessons. "Acts of God" accusations are illogical in light of the efforts to rid societies of all references to God. Therefore, blame now is falling more on "mother nature," eliminating God's participation and then denying its significance as warning and/or judgment.

Remember, Satan is called the "prince of the power of the air," and he has limited power to disturb the atmosphere. However, as much as we would like to, we cannot blame Satan for all the bad. Disobedience, ignorance or lack of wisdom can move us out from under God's protective "umbrella." Satan's M.O. is to bring destruction and death. Humans were given free will to either fight the enemy's opposition with God's help, or to walk about dazed and defeated. The main causes for trouble are:

— Satan's attacks,
— uninformed or foolish decisions,
— spiritual deafness,
— outright rebellion against God,
— judgments from God for correction ("attention-getters")

God's judgments are meant to grab attention to things requiring correction. It is exactly like an earthly parent repeatedly correcting a child with continued and/or increasingly stringent discipline until lessons are learned. Truly, God's judgments originate from His amazing love, because He does not want human beings destroyed through ignorance and rebellion. These facts are a complete study in itself. Once more, easy theology: God is 100 percent good; Satan is 100 percent evil.

What Waits?

If you track current news, you will detect "clouds of warning on the horizon." Increasing intensity and frequency of natural catastrophes such as earthquakes, record floods, droughts, super storms and more have produced fear and a sense of doomsday. Underlying anxiety that things are not right spawns dread of some major disaster happening. Many took seriously the Mayan Calendar as a doomsday prophecy about the end of the world—to their shame. Just look at the recent films and TV programs focusing on these issues. Worldwide famine, disease, major disasters, terrorism and economic cliffs are challenging humanity like never before.

Scared or Prepared?

Mentioning these things is not meant to scare you, but to *prepare* you. Scripture warns about the "beginning of sorrows" (Matthew 24:32-51) to come on the Earth before or as part of the predicted tribulation (Revelation 5-18). It is also called "Jacob's trouble (Jeremiah 30:7)," meaning concentrated, severe difficulties for Israel that impact the entire world.

Jesus referred to this as "the beginning of sorrows (Matthew 24:8)" as a period of severe trouble (we may already be there) with increasing disasters and intensifying difficulties in many arenas of life. However, the predicted *great* tribulation of the Lord's judgment will unleash horrendous, terrifying natural disasters and intense demonic activity never before seen on Earth.

Because this information is in God's infallible Word, it *will* happen. Which side we will be on depends upon our responses to His beckoning—now. Comparing scriptures leads to the strong evidence that these severe events are judgments from God on the downward spiral of morality and the cultural rejection of the one true God. He longs for us to learn the truth about Him and return to Him.

Hope

Prediction of weather patterns has improved with sophisticated instruments to prepare us for physical weather events, and we have God's Word to prepare for "spiritual weather" experiences as well. A predicted "escape" of the future judgment will include all true disciples of Christ Jesus to avoid some or all of the great tribulation.

When we see these difficulties and disasters increase in intensity and frequency, look up to the Lord, give Him your life and stay close to Him, for deliverance is near (Luke 21:28). Absolutely the safest place possible is *in* the Lord where no fear dwells. The timing of this escape, known as the *rapture* or *catching away* has been purposely hidden from believers. The message is to be prepared, not scared.

Knowledge of God's Word and a close fellowship with Him will move us into His secret place—the hiding place till the storms of life pass by or until we are rescued (Psalm 91:1-2).

The Door, Not a Window

All—repeat—all people are immensely valuable to the Lord and He wants *all* to be with Him in eternity. However, we come to Him by following His directions found in His Word. Sadly, many reject Him by taking their own path in life through human reasoning.

Heaven has only one entrance to us mortals on this planet. The Lord Jesus said, "I am the door. If anyone enters by Me, he will be saved, and will go in and out and find pasture (John 10:9)" The Door to heaven will open only through accepting Jesus as Lord and Savior, because He is the Door. Most peep through the "window" of heaven, but neglect to walk through the Door.

So, which metaphor—positive or negative—for clouds has been most prominent in your life? Is there anything you can change if the greater percentage of clouds is negative? What will your choices be for your future?

Moral Of The Story

— *Practical lesson:* Enjoy skyscapes.
— *Spiritual lesson:* God will not condemn you when you ask for wisdom. He gives it freely (James 1:5-7). You are not required to suffer alone.

What other lessons might be contained in this devotional?

Part B—Forest Primeval

A Creative Look at Society
One Long Allegory

Pine Cone

Again, To All Truth Seekers

· ·

*Life is like a pine cone. It may be prickly,
but the growth potential is mighty high.*

· ·

Primeval: pri·me·val; prī-'mē-vəl; adjective; very old or ancient, belonging to the earliest time, primal, early, primitive, primordial.[1]

Be Courageous.

The challenge continues not to believe everything we read or are taught as absolute truth without seriously questioning, investigating and comparing trustworthy sources. This old world is glutted with human-generated ideas and only portions are absolute truth that apply to all people.

Subjective truth clings to personal ideas, suppositions and beliefs *not* applicable to all. This section will call attention to some current faulty attitudes and belief systems promoted by social pressure (the "P. C. police") and will provide more than a nudge—an increasing momentum—toward truth or to confirm what you know already is true.

Truth versus Lies

White and black colors are accepted psychological and universal metaphors for light versus dark, positive versus negative, good versus evil and truth versus lies. Everyone with a functioning conscience would agree truth is good and lies are evil. Therefore, for the sake of discussion, assign the color white to truth and the color black to lies. This analogy applies only to ideas and concepts.

Mixing white and black paint produces shades of gray. Likewise, a mixture of good and evil, truth and error produces polluted "gray thinking," clouded with the fog of confusion. This section exposes

---

1. *By permission. From Merriam-Webster's Collegiate® Dictionary, 11th Edition ©* **2015** by Merriam-Webster, Inc. (www.Merriam-Webster.com)."

more lies and common misconceptions lurking in foggy ideas. Keep your heart open to always question current trends.

Truth is not relative or subjective (ideas adhering to personal preferences). Truth is absolute, i.e. truth applies to all people and laws of the universe, such as gravity. A search for truth will take a lifetime, because we are finite. However, *the path to truth can be found that leads to continued learning*. Finding truth is not just a mental understanding but involves the heart and soul—the inner being—the essence—the real person. The journey is endless because truth is a cosmic matter of the greatest magnitude.

Why This Allegory?

Although the word *primeval* implies no presence or influence of people, you will quickly discover this forest has been polluted by human ideas and philosophies. Some of these are major social, economic, governmental and religious belief systems that are actual hot spots in current world events. "We the people" tend to drift toward convenience and ease, which leads to ignoring some alarming and destructive issues now embedded in modern cultures. A significant percentage of humanity is "wising up" and beginning to challenge the status quo.

Question Everything.

Are you positive you have been taught truth? Are you willing to die for what you currently believe? Remember, it is possible to die for something you sincerely believe is truth, *whether or not it is true*. Truth is an issue about intellectual honesty involving the heart while comparing information with Scripture. Unless all possibilities are filtered through this discernment process with no preconceived agenda, an informed decision about what truth is cannot be made. Engage your mind in this stimulating adventure. God gave us brains and expects us to use them honestly!

Enjoy and think!

1

Newcomers

· ·
Something new is not always better.
· ·

During an unusually dry season, a grass fire rampaged through a small community causing moderate damage, but much fear. Although no loss of life occurred, many terrified pets scattered to surrounding areas. Searches for pets ensued and all dogs and cats were located, but a pair of peacocks, Henry and Henrietta, could not be found.

Peacocks announce their presence with raucous "pea-kaaaawk" calls. This pair was so traumatized by the fire and other bolting pets that they were speechless. Fleeing in desperation and fear, they paid no attention to their direction or distance, found what they thought was a hiding place in a forest and settled in stealthily.

However, the local residents, overwhelmed by curiosity, began investigating as word spread of their presence. Intrepid rabbits tiptoed to visual range, coyotes crept within sniffing distance and bear cubs climbed nearby pines to peer down at the newcomers.

The peacocks realized they were exposed as other forest creatures began to encircle them, so they emerged from hiding and attempted to demonstrate fearlessness. The forest citizens had not seen creatures like this and were astonished at the stunning colors of the male's audacious tail feathers. The peacocks had never seen forest creatures either, were wide-eyed and breathing shallowly but did not let on.

A cougar, an obvious leader, walked boldly to the peacock pair and announced, "Welcome to our Forest!" His typical, screeching feline voice sounded more like a warning than a welcome.

From the perception of threat, the peacocks found their voices, and both blurted out in their unique, alarming and blaring language, "Pea-kaaawwk, pea-kaaawwk, pea-kaaawwk!" All animals fled

"Welcome to the Forest!"

in terror including the cougar. Exceedingly pleased, Henry spread his showy tail feathers and proudly strutted in the weeds with Henrietta at his side.

The worried forest occupants gathered to decide what to do about the newcomers. Making no effort to hide his suspicion, the eldest squirrel sneered, "These whatever-they-are are too different and don't speak our language! And, they are waaaaaay too loud. Very disturbing, if you ask me. I vote they be driven out pronto!" The entire squirrel community chattered agreement.

All rabbits in a huddle were nervous about what these creatures eat and selected the boldest Jack to represent them, who piped up excitedly, "These are way too strange to be birds—they might be dangerous dinosaurs! We think caution is in order here because they're scary and they must be up to no good. We don't want those creatures snooping around our nests and burrows, no sireeee!" All rabbits wiggled noses and nodded.

Raucous crows, always ready to speak anything anytime and

excited by the challenge to have newcomers to heckle, chorused almost in unison, "We just need to get to know them before voting. They might actually be assets to the forest."

Mumbling in their respective corners, turkeys and buzzards were openly jealous of the bright showy feathers, called them intruders and passed a block vote to drive the disgustingly prideful creatures back to wherever they came from.

Coyotes and foxes all agreed to let them stay, recognizing their identity as birds. A few furtive, hushed voices conferred among themselves, "They probably lay giant eggs. In fact, they look plump enough to make a meal of them right now." One quickly retorted in a stage whisper, "We should eat the eggs, not the source. Besides, it would be downright illegal," generating some muffled snickers among the carnivores within hearing range.

The stolid bears did not care since the unnamed creatures were no threat to them. They leisurely sat munching berries and just watched, sleepy from having already helped themselves to generous portions of the refreshments and being gassy to the open objection of those nearby. Other groups made split decisions. All agreed to meet again soon.

The second gathering was nearly as indecisive. After lengthy deliberation, only three things were agreed upon: they needed a name for these creatures, they all needed to practice tolerance and the leaders should make all the decisions.

Hadley Hawk proposed, "I think the name "peacock" is fitting since it sounds like their language." All marveled at the idea as inspired, his approval rating dramatically increased and he was unanimously elected Councilman. No one realized that now four decision-makers, King Caldwell Cougar, Duke Morris Moose, Bishop Otto Owl and the new Councilman Hadley Hawk might produce a split decision.

For some time, Bishop Owl had preached to and pressured the forest citizens toward tolerance as the only way to get along with so many diverse occupants. Since the Bishop was highly respected as the wisest member of the forest, they had been gradually adopting his philosophy of tolerating diverse beliefs and ways of life to the point of actually accepting and blending many opposing ideas. A small number of rabbits even dared to nervously dig their burrows next door to the coyotes—but only once. The citizens understood Bishop Owl to mean all systems were of equal value and to be adopted or at least agreed with. The result was just as diverse as the different beliefs had always been, each inventing their own blend. The Bishop restated his tolerance doctrine to the enthusiastic approval of most attendees. A few deer remained distant and silent.

During this time, Henry and Henrietta grew hungry and began looking for food, pecking in the weeds but found the seeds to be low quality. They recognized the unfriendliness of some forest creatures but were not worried about the meeting's result. At their old residence, they had intimidated and eventually subdued barking dogs and teasing cats and were confident they could do it with these inferior forest critters. All they had to do was threaten with their loud voices.

"Just think," stated Henry, "our new situation with these stupid creatures might be much better than we had at our old home. No one will bother us."

"The seeds here so far aren't as tasty and quite disappointing," complained Henrietta.

"But we excel at intimidation tactics and it will be fun to try them here," protested Henry enthusiastically. "Look, we've already seen a demonstration of how easy it is to scare them."

Henry and Henrietta began immediately developing a plan for better nutrition for the entire forest, especially their favorite seeds. They also decided to condescend and speak Forest instead of their native language.

The third meeting took place in the wild persimmon grove and included only the ruling class: King Cougar, Duke Moose, Bishop Owl and Councilman Hawk. Much time was wasted debating the peacock's shocking language, concluding the only reasonable solution was for speaking Forest to be mandatory, unaware the peacocks had already made that decision. Rules of order disintegrated into arguing about old social issues they had hoped would never be addressed again. Bishop Owl reaffirmed continuing the tolerance policy by accepting the unpopular peacocks. Duke Moose then complained of a headache coming on

Council Meeting

from so much thinking.

Swaggering with his newly recognized brilliance, Councilman Hawk raised the issue of the carnivore regulation. "Allow me to humbly remind you, honorable King Cougar, that learning to respect the herbivores has been an extremely difficult task for you and other carnivores." Hadley secretly hunted outside the forest.

A law was already in place restricting the carnivores to only one serving of meat a week and only as population control of the more prolific breeders. The community had effectively squelched a few brief rebellions. King Cougar was elected on the "respect for all" platform and was trying to be the example for all carnivores of a law-abiding citizen.

Duke Moose quietly suggested, "Councilman Hawk is correct, you know. The peacocks' presence would be too much temptation for the weaker members of your race and could result in profiling and prosecution of upstanding citizens."

The King responded to this reminder, and unwilling to lose his position as king finally voted to expel them. The Duke's headache was now throbbing and he declined to vote. Councilman Hawk was overjoyed that he would now have the swing vote.

Bishop Owl, always ready to preach, challenged the King's vote, "The peacocks are just different, but quite beautiful. Perhaps their beauty means they are superior and would be assets to the forest when we get to know them." He had conversed with the crows. "We have always welcomed and accepted new residents wholeheartedly, and the forest has ample space and food sources to accommodate all races." He warned, "I urge you all to just think of the trouble it might cause if we vote them out. Others in the community would fear that they too could be voted out. Not good for community morale. We also might be accused of being racist."

King Cougar and Duke Moose were finally persuaded by the logic and tolerance of Bishop Owl and voted to allow the peacocks to stay. The ruling class would not admit they were secretly afraid of the peacocks. They did realize their need to officially ratify the tolerance doctrine for future newcomers so tough decisions like this could be avoided. Relieved that this ordeal was over, Duke Moose went home immediately to chew willow bark and recuperate.

In the meantime, Henry and Henrietta had decided to tough it out with the forest residents by demonstrating their way of life is best and the forest citizens were clueless about how to do things right. They had great plans of election to office and transforming the forest society with new regs and were confident they could rule by fear. Besides, the route home was a mystery.

• •

The Real Definition

Have you heard the expression, "If you stand for nothing, you will fall for anything"? If your belief system is shaky, you can be easily swayed to believe and adopt anything, including opposing ideas, through fear of persecution.

Did the forest residents know the true definition of tolerance? Incorrect understanding left the forest vulnerable to manipulation by the Bishop and the peacocks' persuasiveness to influence them without knowing their agenda. The forest understood Bishop Owl's teaching of tolerance to mean acceptance and even adoption of diverse and perhaps opposing ideas with all systems of equal value to society. Do you recognize this ideology in modern cultures? Do you agree or disagree with it?

Tolerance is a current cultural mantra. Many people who complain about others being intolerant fail to recognize they are just as guilty if not more so. Its usage has changed over the years from being a "live and let live" attitude to now mean excluding and even vilifying those who differ from the mainstream opinions. We should be polite to all, be able to have our own opinions and not be required to join the "group-think." Fear now accompanies the new version of tolerance due to political correctness expressed in persecution.

Tolerance Applied Intolerantly

Tolerance now is applied increasingly and intolerantly toward Christianity—a belief system different from all other beliefs. *True* Christianity tolerates other systems, never applies force or forbids others from believing what they want to believe. The Inquisition, witch-hunts, burning crosses on the lawns of African Americans and such are *not* examples of *true* Christianity in action. Just think for a moment about other belief systems that do force themselves on others, either by threat of severe restriction of freedoms, torture or death. The lack of information about what individual religions and social systems really promote and reject leads to misunderstanding and misapplying tolerance.

The Trend

Recent laws have been passed that restrict only Christianity and not other belief systems—not even the systems that threaten loss of freedoms or death. Other belief systems are allowed all kinds of public freedom, and more restrictions are imposed on Christians to the point where incrimination can be the result if we state our beliefs publicly. True Christianity does not force anyone else to accept the doctrines. The Word of God convicts and they are thereby offended, fearful, and sling accusations of hate speech. The United States Constitution defines and guarantees true freedom, equal opportunities for success, and tolerance for all to include:

— the right to work hard toward success,
— the right to be as sane or crazy as you want to be as long as no one is hurt or unreasonably restricted,

— the right to believe any ol' way you want to believe,
— the right to express beliefs and opinions freely as long as good manners are in place, beliefs are not forced on others and are not treason.

The Constitution does not guarantee
equality *of income or services.*

Disagreeing Agreeably

Voicing disagreements agreeably is a sign of a healthy society in striving for truth and what works best, but only if we practice our disagreements without being disagreeable. Differences morphing into attacks against people instead of ideas, clearly demonstrate the absence of real tolerance. Listen closely to some of the speeches that criticize other people. When their arguments are weak, they attack character instead of policies.

In this current global trend toward polarization of opinions and beliefs, I believe it is critical that we solidify precisely what we believe and why. Many people are uninformed about what true Christianity is. Clarify your beliefs by questioning yourself:

— What do I really believe and not believe?
— If I dislike Christianity, is it because I have met people who call themselves Christians, but do not behave like it?
— Is my rejection of Christianity because I have never read the Bible or know what true Christianity is?
— If I wear the Christian label, do I really know the truth about and in Christianity?

Moral Of The Story

— *Practical lesson:* Practice true tolerance that does not restrict, devalue or ridicule any person.
— *Spiritual lesson:* Do not fear finding error in your belief system. Rejoice for correction when it happens.

What other lessons might be contained here?

2

One Size Fits All

• •

One size for all is a poor fit.

• •

The prideful, manipulating peacocks were successful in their coup of the forest for a few years. They shrewdly instigated many new restrictions, some of them opposing existing regulations that caused great confusion. King Cougar was losing his influence.

Rebellion brewed quietly with mild complaining, progressing to open arguments, then outright shouting matches. None of the issues were addressing the causes of the complaints, and they were flinging unfounded accusations at each other instead.

King Cougar suddenly understood the problems after living in a fog of confusion, decided to be kingly again and called a meeting to inform the citizens that this kind of behavior, if not curtailed or redirected, would lead to full-blown civil war and total destruction of forest life. The peacocks had actually usurped some of the king's authority, so he had some issues to address. He enlightened them with his evaluation of the difficulties and was able to clarify the situation to the disgruntled groups who had been quarreling between and among their clans. He pointed out, "The peacocks are definitely the culprits, and if they will repent of their pride and let the forest return to the pre-peacock condition, all will be well."

Relieved to have a focus to attack instead of each other, the forest turned their full attention to Henry and Henrietta with loud railing. After screeching at his top volume, King Cougar was able to startle the forest into silence. With gruffness and deep emotion he spoke, "We know better than to act this way! Stop this now! We must restore decency and courtesy!"

Many hung their heads in contrition. All was quiet in the forest for the first time in weeks. The king's voice softened, "Now this is better!" He went on to explain the why and how of the forest difficulties and was actually making more sense than Bishop Owl ever had. "Go home and rest. Come back tomorrow to peacefully discuss solutions for our communities."

A new and calmer atmosphere prevailed at the next gathering. The now courageous king was able to confirm for the citizens that the peacocks must be issued an ultimatum: repent of pride, relinquish control or leave.

Of course, Henry and Henrietta refused, feeling superior to the uproar, insisting their way was the only way, and the forest simply needed to be reasonable. "None of you understands what's best for you!" exclaimed Henry. "We can clear up any misunderstanding. Just give us a chance to address your grievances."

Concerned the peacocks would dupe the citizens again, King Cougar shook his head silently but his gesture was not necessary. "No," he replied calmly, "we don't want your leadership any more! You've already created too much havoc by confusing our laws and regulations to the point we don't even know if we're doing something illegal. We have much to undo."

The forest was unanimously on to them now, finally realizing nothing would improve with the peacocks still insisting on their way. With new understanding, they expressed their disgust over the peacocks' pride and their we-know-what's-best-for-you attitude. They banded together as a solid unit forcing Henry and Henrietta to leave immediately "or else."

Henry and Henrietta suddenly realized the forest citizens were no longer afraid of them. Since they had not multiplied—their eggs kept disappearing despite all the regulations in place protecting them. Besides, they were too busy meddling in forest matters to raise a family. They spouted petulantly, "We hate it here anyway! We'll just find a better place where we'll be appreciated and can raise a family in peace!" Henry and Henrietta stomped away holding heads high and tail feathers displayed in undaunted pride. The wily coyotes and foxes were disappointed but kept quiet about losing their secret egg source. The rest of the forest residents cheered.

A spontaneous celebration erupted after the peacocks' departure with the bears eating more than their share of refreshments and being gassy as usual. No one complained, just distanced themselves.

The forest occupants felt empowered over the peacock expulsion and began raising issues to be changed. At a meeting of interested citizens, King Cougar addressed his greatest personal concern. "I think it's high time to do away with the restrictions on meat consumption for carnivores. It's unnatural and puts a greater hardship on carnivores than any other group."

All rodents, outnumbering other forest races by a wide margin and high on the food chain, hollered in unison, "NO!" causing an echo through the trees. All were silent for a moment stunned by the decibels.

A large raccoon complained, "Hey, rodents should only have half a vote since they have breeding advantages." That too was shouted down at the same volume.

Caldwell Cougar, becoming weary of all the turmoil and realizing his kingly influence was quickly diminishing, spent his days sulking and complaining about the "No" vote. He eventually fell out of favor and resigned to join his cousins in the mountains. Hadley Hawk was exposed as being too indecisive about all issues to represent any group and decided to relocate to his secret hunting ground.

Morris Moose's persistent headaches from too much thinking nudged him into retirement to become nearly a recluse. Otto Owl, having preached himself hoarse, became rather ineffective and tiresome. He also retired with a pension of mice delivered twice weekly in outrageous defiance of the regulation restricting carnivores.

The forest society was left leaderless long enough for civility to further decline. The former leadership had left many unresolved and confusing issues, so they rejected having any leaders and let the forest run itself. They began to ignore some regulations causing great fear and uncertainty. A small group of animals worried that the situation was becoming critical, and they united with one purpose: to plan a better environment. They brainstormed ideas, beginning to feel hopeful that their society could return to sanity.

The eldest bear, speaking for all bears suggested, "There aren't enough berry bushes, so we think at least half the trees should be cut down to make room for more berries. Leave the fruit and honey bee trees, of course."

Rabbits, communicating in their squeaky nose-wiggling, gave a signal that they were ready to speak in Forest language, "We like the idea of berry bushes but we think vegetable gardens are better." They enthusiastically began planning burrows directly under the vegetable roots and calling the network "The Cabbage Patch Gang."

Birds were concerned their nesting areas would be too scarce with fewer trees, and nests in gardens and berry bushes would be too vulnerable to being trampled by nibbling rabbits and berry picking bears.

A bobcat protested in his attention-getting high pitch, "Look at the size of these plump bears! They already have enough berries, and besides, they're too gassy and are polluting the air!" A chorused agreement followed, dramatically covering noses and fanning the air with paws.

Squirrels objected loudly to cutting trees, chattering that they needed their acrobatic equipment to stay in shape. The deer thought ahead about trying to secure their newborns under thorny bushes and cabbage leaves and emphatically opposed all suggestions. No environmental changes were agreed upon. They did, however, elect representatives to research all possibilities for improvement.

The assembly of the elected representatives was disorderly. A few delegates had not done their research but had strong opinions and believed they already had the necessary information. A group of bears lobbied and managed to persuade a few delegates. Several beavers, always difficult to understand because of their toothy lisp, tried to communicate their concern, "Fwe think iff's a bvad itfdea thu elimfinathe any twees aft all or difertf any fwater for busfthes and garftens." Few could decipher.

The majority of opinions were to table all the motions and reconvene after all the delegates had done proper research. They began thinking having a leader would be a good idea.

At the next convergence, a handsome fox with a gorgeous rusty red coat stood up and suggested, "Why don't we elect one of us to make the decisions for all and to make the necessary changes to restore the forest." All thought that was a nifty idea since agreement had become so difficult and tiresome. Heated discussion ensued about who would be the fairest.

Mr. S. Fox then delivered his speech, "We need a capable leader, one who loves *all* trees, *all* berry bushes, *all* beaver dams, and *all* gardens, and who will be fair to *all*. I believe I qualify. I *love* the forest and *everyone* here." All agreed the good-looking fox would best serve them, since he was convincing, was a clever fellow and had thought of the idea. The fox was unanimously elected president on the platform of change, fairness and hope. All were quite relieved to have made a decision.

A Foxy Speech

President Fox was delighted with his power to appoint assistants and impose regulations for all arenas of forest life. They were to be enforced immediately by the newly formed Badger Militia and Weasel Tax Collectors. All forest citizens protested the taxes and regulations, but these had become law without their knowledge.

Unhappy, displaced beavers grumbled, "Fsno one lisfthenefth. Our racfthe ifth dthoomedtf!" No jobs for them were available except as tree cutters to make room for more berry bushes and veggie gardens, watered by a new canal that nearly depleted the beaver pond. The now declared the leadership and had crossed a red teeth and boldly staged a protest.

angry beavers bravely was abusing the forest line. They gritted their

Beavers Lose

All tree dwellers were ordered to build apartment nests to consolidate space. Rabbits were forced to occupy only hollow spaces in the uncut trees.and to never dig under the veggies. Each race was assigned a portion of a garden or berry bush and was ordered never to trade or sell their sections. Meat regulations were reinforced, except for Otto Owl's retirement pension. All had to eat more veggies and berries to stay healthy.

President S. Fox presented himself as the first to comply when he demonstrated with great pomp and drama his enjoyment of green beans, sweet potatoes and lettuce. The enraptured audience was blind to his award-winning performance of eating only one bite of each. However, fresh duck was regularly smuggled into his den by some clever raccoons wanting to gain the president's favor. No one seemed to notice his weight gain. Many sneaky raccoons were appointed Secret Service agents. Hiding behind their masks, they pretended to be friends of the forest and reveled in their new power. These spies reported so many regulation violators that new jails were built and fenced with newly cut trees. Over-crowding became an issue.

Citizens considered dangerous (porcupines, venomous snakes and such) were ordered to live in ghettos on the forest outskirts, never to breach their borders above or below ground or be fined, shamefully returned, jailed or sentenced to death. To enforce, every underground burrow was filled in at the borders, and all border trees and bushes were cut down so that no ghetto occupant could sneak across undetected. Displaced non-threatening citizens vociferously protested about this inconvenience without prior notice. Many underground and aboveground citizens were trapped in the new ghettos due to their inattention to the political atmosphere. Their appeals to the president were ignored, and they were suddenly thrust into the lawlessness of the ghettos and back in their positions in the food chain.

Theft became particularly troublesome, as rats and mice were determined not to pay taxes and went into hiding underground, emerging at night to steal food. Fighting among the population rose again, and the first riot ended in the destruction of two gardens. President S. Fox appointed his relatives as judges who were soon overwhelmed by complaints, lawsuits and crime cases.

All forest inhabitants began to understand the source of their problems—the lies they had swallowed. They secretly complained and rued the day they gave one individual authority over all. They wanted their forest back, but it had become illegal to congregate. Many dissidents went underground where rats and mice were hiding and who gladly joined the rebellion. All quill weapons had been confiscated with regulations disallowing replacement. However, that did not affect the lawbreakers, who simply hid unregistered weapons. The rebellion was hesitant to let outlaws join due to distrust, although they had a large stash of quills. What to do? This was not the change, fairness and hope they wanted or had been promised. Disillusionment became intense discontent.

• •

Exemptions to Equality

It should be obvious that regulations interfering with every aspect of life and requiring equality in every area will not work smoothly if at all. Only a select few individuals benefit, such as the elites who make the rules and then vote exemptions for themselves. The U. S. Constitution is unique compared with past national governments, because it guarantees equal *chances* for "life, liberty, and the *pursuit* of happiness." This means individuals have the right to live freely and the right to chase after contentment as long as it does not infringe on someone else's rights. It does not say that happiness is a *right* guaranteed by government or that equality means everyone having the same things or the same services. We have the same opportunities to these benefits.

Individual initiative turns the wheels of successful societies. Past political promises declared government would provide a "chicken in every pot and a car in every garage." This catchy declaration is credited to President Herbert Hoover, but was never spoken by him. Instead, the Republican Party placed it in ads for his election. This promise is perhaps the beginning of a political trend toward entitlements and the philosophy of uniformity, and if left unchecked, will stall or stop national economic success.

Women's clothing was available in "One Size Fits All" until changed to just "One Size" and is appropriate primarily for the plus sizes. Even the changed label does not apply to all sizes and calls our attention to the fact that the word "fits" is flexible. Therefore, the label "One Size Fits All" and "One Size" are lies pertaining to clothing and many other life issues. Some political systems try to squeeze the masses into a one-size mold. Question everything.

Uniformity

The cultural pressure of having the same opinions, speaking the same, requiring the same services for all, having equal incomes (except for the elite) and having the same belief systems will not produce a perfect social structure. One size for all is a poor fit. The result will always be people on the losing side of having equal rights. The beavers were the biggest losers. Government trends in the western world are definitely toward socialism, communism and uniformity, and some have been there for a while already. Do we really want it? If we do, then it appears we could be on the winning side. If we oppose it, what can we do? "Socialism is a philosophy of failure, the creed of ignorance and the gospel of envy; its inherent virtue is the equal sharing of misery"—Winston Churchill.[1]

So, whom do we believe and what do we trust in this unstable world of lies? Culture has been programming the populace for years to believe without question what they are taught. I say, along with a growing multitude, intensely question everything!

Look Ahead

If you want to know the future, turn to Scripture. Bible prophecy has never been wrong. End-times descriptions are presented both metaphorically and literally, and comparing Old and New Testament prophecies presents a clearer picture of what lies in store for the creaking and deteriorating world's systems. So many steps are in place already leading toward a one-world government that returning wholly to our individual freedoms may be a difficult, painful and lengthy process, if it is even possible.

Why has socialism gained such a strong foothold? This humanist philosophy has many dangerous tentacles with varied causes and alarming effects:

- the expectation of free stuff,
- socialist instructors' agendas,
- years of little or no instruction about God,
- evolution refuting God's involvement in the Earth and humanity, robbing us of purpose in life,
- attack against any mention of God in public life,
- growing belief that there is no God,
- belief that humans are gods,

---

1. In a speech: The First Conservative Election Broadcast, 4 June 1945. Quoted in *Capet*, Charlot & Hill. 201-2.

— growing belief that all religions are of equal value (except
Christianity that doesn't "fit in").

Widespread now are unreliable beliefs in self and political
ideologies as answers to humanity's dilemmas. Displaced are sound
beliefs in God and truth about Him, resulting in a severely cracked
moral foundation dangerous for national survival. Many now are
adhering to beliefs and opinions that good and evil are only concepts
of the mind, that there is no right or wrong—only gray areas of
relativism, and if there is a God, then He is all love and no
justice. Those mind sets leave us bobbing like a cork on murky ocean
surf—no specific direction, no vision, no stability. Our confused
social condition and religious thought has *traded personal beliefs
and opinions* for absolute truth.

Remember the definition of truth—something that correlates to
what actually is and applies to everyone. Truth is absolute. Beliefs
and opinions are often founded on faulty or incomplete information
and personal preferences leading to dangerous deceptions. Seeking
absolute truth is vital, so make it a life-long quest. One size does not
fit all.

Moral Of The Story
— *Practical lesson:* Question everything you read and hear;
thoroughly investigate the sources.
— *Spiritual lesson:* The Lord is the same yesterday, today and
forever (Hebrews 13:8). He can be trusted completely
because He does not change.

What other lessons might be contained in this installment?

3

Reign Of Confusion

•••••••••••••••••••••••••

Choose help from one who
sees the big picture.

•••••••••••••••••••••••••••

The forest citizens had dug what looked like a bottomless social pit—so deep they could not find a solution without total organized rebellion. President S. Fox was so satisfied with his set-up that he was unaware of the rampant discontent in the social and political structures. The citizens covertly discussed their need to congregate secretly and to devise strategies.

They chose an abandoned underground burrow as the safest location. The only animals that could meet without their absence being noticed or could even fit underground were smaller animals, lizards and birds. All insects declined the invitation, concerned they would be inadvertently crushed in the gatherings, but avowed to annoy the establishment. A few verified anti-president raccoons, badgers and weasels were allowed. Plans were discussed about enlarging their location to accommodate more dissidents. An unidentified voice was heard from the back, "We could use an abandoned badger hole." The crowd nearly roared, "That's what we're using now!" Then they all cowered upon realizing how loud their outburst was. Everyone remained silent for several minutes to listen for snoops above ground in case escape was necessary.

One of the anti-Fox raccoons timidly suggested, "There aren't enough of us to fight this system. Let's invite the non-venomous snakes. They'll fit underground and will add to our ranks." The idea was quickly dismissed because of the serpents' forked tongue reputation and disobedient appetite for rodents. Only the residents who had been hinting at solutions were allowed.

• • • • •

Chief Rushing Wind of the Forest Bald Eagle Tribe had been observing the entire situation over the years from his eyrie at the top of the tallest pine. The forest citizens were oblivious to his presence, and without detection, his eagle eye and acute hearing took in every detail of their predicament. The exponential growth of regulations imposed on the forest had squeezed the population into unnatural molds. Confusion and frustration were high. The Chief wondered if they would even receive suggestions from one who could see the whole picture from above. He waited for the perfect opportunity to intervene.

• • • • •

The underground movement began in earnest when one of the squirrels, Ragged Tail, was arrested emerging from a ground hole. He was questioned intensively with threat of torture to reveal why he had been in the ground instead of in his tree nest. The hapless squirrel was so flustered that he spoke incoherently. No dissidents had discussed what to say if caught. He fainted from terror of possible torture and was taken to a jail cage, cleverly constructed by Secret Service raccoons' dexterous fingers. Poor Ragged revived

Ragged Tail's Fright

and tried to protest. He was left on his own with a warning, "Don't even *think* about an escape!"

President S. Fox was informed and chided, "This situation needs a more gentle approach. You boys are just too heavy-handed." He considered them obtuse and needed training in persuasion techniques. However, he was glad the squirrel had been softened-up.

After two days with no nourishment, the incarcerated squirrel began begging for food. He had thought of a perfect defense: he is really a ground squirrel and has not yet adjusted to tree nests, which was true. That sounded perfectly logical and believable, and he was confident of his release.

President Fox paid a visit bringing the best acorns, nuts and seeds and greeted him reassuringly. The president poured on his charm and chatted calmly, "I apologize profusely for your distress caused by this inconvenience. I will see to it that matters will be speedily concluded and you will be released."

Ragged was completely disarmed and forgot his perfect defense. He visibly relaxed and revealed his name, beginning to believe he had totally misjudged this president. After all, he had never met the president in person until now and he was overwhelmed. They chatted about the forest, their families, what they liked and how they occupied their time. Ragged Tail let slip that he had attended meetings to improve the environment. The sly president, sounding impressed and interested, continued pumping him for information. Ragged began squirming, realizing he had blown it. He worried about being considered a traitor, so he thought quickly enough to give false locations for their meetings. The president promised to set in motion Ragged's release from jail.

President Fox immediately ordered the Badger Militia and Raccoon Secret Service to investigate and search for unusually busy ground holes. A few holes were investigated but digging produced no congregations of rebels. The now agitated President Fox ordered the Secret Service raccoons to be on high alert at night, which would logically be the time of their greatest rebellious activity.

The president revisited the incarcerated Ragged but this time with a different face. He was not calm or reassuring and stated firmly, "Mr. Ragged Tail, you are in serious trouble! We searched all the places you identified and found no pockets of rebellion. What do you say to that? Huh?"

The distressed Ragged Tail, noting the change in the president's demeanor nervously replied, "They constantly change locations not to be caught."

A Visit From the President

President Fox took notice that Ragged did not clearly align himself with him nor reject the rebellion. "I seeeeeeeeeeeeeeee. . .," he uttered almost inaudibly. "Do you know what I'm going to do?" He spoke deliberately with increasing volume, "I'm going to keep on looking till we find every last rebel in this forest! No more special treats for you!" His last words were shouted. The president's threats so alarmed Ragged that he fainted again.

The president immediately summoned all the Militia, Secret Service and Tax Collectors and charged them to find the rebels or not be paid, be fired and imprisoned. Some badgers and raccoons had become disillusioned and ineffective, were quite afraid of the consequences of not fulfilling their duties, so they decided to lay low and strategize their own mutiny. The Weasel Tax Collectors protested that they were only bean counters, not experienced investigators. President Fox confined them to house arrest until the roundup of all dissidents.

Because the underground was kept busy moving their meetings, they achieved little progress. One of the rabbits, Hopalong, out of sheer boredom began enlarging his tunnel and managed to unplug it under the porcupine ghetto border, popped his head up and to his surprise, startled a porcupine into shooting some quills. Hopalong wiggled his nose excitedly and managed to squeak, "Hello there!

What've you guys been doing?"

"What do you think we've been doing?" asked the incredulous and angry Stickers. "Look what you've done to us! Our living conditions are deplorable here! Absolute lawlessness!"

Hopalong was unsure what that meant but sensed the negative tone and replied, "But we didn't do it! President Fox and his cronies did all this! And the administrations before that too! Us rabbits always got along with you prickly guys, so don't blame us! Our lives aren't easy either. We have soooooooo many laws and sooooooo much anger and confusion. We sure could use some help!"

"Why should we help you?" puffed Stickers. "No one has helped us." He paused a moment before speaking again, "I suppose we'll consider helping if you promise to help us. Give me time to talk to my family and friends and see what they say." Stickers glumly waddled away. Hopalong was left alone wondering what to do. He waited quite a while, but upon realizing the danger of his accidental position, decided to return underground to let everyone know he had dug through and they might get some help. He was beginning to feel a shred of hope. Just as he started down his hole, he remembered the quills lying on the ground and scooped them up.

• •

Possible Scenarios

How would you like this allegory to end? The most serious scenario would be devastation and loss of life. Citizens could become so desperate they would not care, making life even more difficult for all. Expansion of the militia would be required and fear would again be the prevailing atmosphere—a scenario replayed in socialist governments with the potential of becoming dictatorships.

The best scenario—replace President S. Fox with a courageous critter to make tough decisions with good moral principles. It is quite unlikely that President Fox would repent of his power grab and reverse all the unnatural regulations imposed under the guise of tolerance, change, fairness and hope. He reveled in his reign.

John E. E. Dalberg-Acton, known as Lord Acton, an English writer, historian and politician of the nineteenth century, astutely stated, "Power tends to corrupt, and absolute power corrupts absolutely."[1] Most individuals who have tasted power do all they can to maintain their positions. Perhaps all the president's employees would hide, not support him or join the rebellion from fear of imprisonment. Mass defections would make holding onto power impossible.

What's Happening?

Taking a hard look at historical and contemporary political and cultural atmospheres across the globe reveals none of us are immune to take-overs. Slavery still exists and dictatorships impose their rules on the common folk. The strong and ruthless conquer the weak wherever and whenever they can, causing oppression and fear.

Competition and pride are innate human desires that can go wild. Idealists who attempt to create the perfect social system inflict severe and unreasonable restrictions on populations. We have observed it in the attempts to make all political "-isms" (communism and such) suitable for all. In the process, many people have been exterminated as unfit for the idealists' version of the perfect utopia—another great fear. The elite at the top enjoy all the benefits of power and wealth.

Who Gets the Blame?

When freedoms are restricted by an overwhelming abundance of laws, confusion reigns. God is not the author of confusion (1 Corinthians 14:33) and shares none of the blame. Confusion is the product of humanity's limited human reasoning influenced by the kingdom of darkness. The sheer volume of regulations produces conflict and uncertainty about what is legal and what is not. Large societies and governments become burdened by their own weight. What seem like good ideas to the select few who make the decisions finally degrade into amoral systems without God's guidance. Human ideas always fall short of God's ways.

The Final Solution

---

1. *The World Book Encyclopedia*. 1991. s.v. "Acton, Lord."

The ultimate lesson to derive from these allegory installments is that *a political solution can never be the final solution.* This lesson will be underscored again as the story continues. Faith must be restored somehow, but faith in what or whom? Faith is not neutral and does not exist without a focus. The focus must not be just concepts or philosophies but must be the only trustworthy higher authority— God.

So, on what is your faith focused? Yourself? Politics—a new election? Popularity? Wealth? All those are faulty and will always fail. Our God, the God of Abraham, Isaac and Jacob, will never fail (Luke 16:17) and He is infinitely more intelligent than the most intelligent human who has ever lived or ever will live! Our God is so very willing to give us wisdom when we get to know Him and can hear and receive His guidance.

Moral Of The Story
— *Practical lesson:* Confusion can only be counteracted with absolute truth.
— *Spiritual lesson:* Faith must travel with truth and hope to focus on God's solutions.

What other lessons might be contained here?

· ·
General Confusion
· ·

Generally, the Generals get around
Wearing a variety of faces.
Hats, name tags and honors abound,
Popping up in general places.
General Nuisance and General Headache are found
With General Area in many spaces.
General Trouble tends to hover and hound;
General Mess and General Chaos cover all bases.

General Store, General Manager, and General Merchandise
Partnered for an illegal business offshore.
General Uproar raised his outcries
And wrote a speech for General Bore.
General Editor was charged to generalize
To the General Assembly to avoid war.
In the melee General Hospital had to apologize
To all Generals, but wasn't sure what it was for.

Diane Shields Spears ©

... 4 ...

Fear versus Faith

· ·
Fearing fear itself is an oxymoron.
· ·

High in his eyrie, Chief Rushing Wind decided the time was right to counsel with his tribe. Soaring high, he announced for all to meet at the forest's NW edge overlooking the venomous snake ghetto where only eagles and hawks would go. They congregated quickly and settled in the trees. The Chief began relating the events since King Cougar's reign. Some eagles were already aware of the situation, but had not desired to do anything, because the venomous snake ghetto was actually an advantage for them, corralling their dinners into one convenient location but all the while becoming lethargic and out of shape from lack of challenge.

Judge Strong Heart Eagle, in charge of the Eagle Court, asked, "Have you devised a plan for restoring the forest to sanity?"

"Yes," the Chief replied, "and I am requesting full participation. We should be able to accomplish

Council of Eagles

· 195 ·

the task without detection. I suggest the first order of business is to rescue Ragged Tail from his cell and then abduct President Fox and scare the be-dickens out of him. We'll decide later about the other incarcerated folk when we determine why they were jailed."

"Well, that sounds all neat and tidy. How do you plan to execute this?" asked Judge Eagle skeptically. "We're going to need a pretty sophisticated strategy to overcome all the forces in place protecting their little kingdom. They've been very thorough."

Some murmuring in the ranks arose about how dangerous this could be. A few spoke outright that it would be impossible and they could be risking their lives.

Reverend Bright Morning Eagle spoke up, "We acknowledge this is a fearful thing, but fearful thinking will get us nowhere. Let's have faith that our source of wisdom, the Supreme-Eagle-in-the-Sky, has the solution. We definitely need to reason together with him before we make any moves."

"Yes, yes," was the subdued response, glad of the reminder.

"I fully understand the risks and I've been well aware of their strategies all along," stated the Chief. "I do have some ideas, so that's why I called you all together. Rescuing Ragged Tail will arouse the opposition, so we must prepare for strong and immediate retaliation from the Badger Militia and Secret Service Raccoons with their quill weapons. If we can manage it silently, we will have several hours to set the other strategies in place before the Militia realizes Ragged is missing. Timing is crucial because they are starving the poor squirrel by allowing him water and meager morsels only after sunrise. He's become weak and will not be able to run. No guards are visible, so they must think no one would value him enough to attempt a jailbreak. We should begin getting some food to him immediately. We have the superior escape advantage, even the slowest of us."

Muffled chuckles arose. All knew the Chief referred to Swifty, so nicknamed as a joke, his given name being White Rapids. Always good-natured, Swifty had accepted it and had transformed it into clowning. In response, he raised his wings and flapped with exaggerated slowness to the delight of all.

The Chief continued, "We do need to be courageous. If we do

nothing, evil will reign and the whole forest will come to ruin."

"OK," responded the Reverend. "How 'bout Clear Water and Thunder to deliver seeds or such tonight? Both slip through the air quietly and always aim accurately."

Chief Rushing Wind continued, "Actually, I was thinking of Angel as the best candidate to handle the food drop and the rescue. She is also silent in the air, agile and breathtakingly quick. I believe she can do it alone, but I will give her the option of selecting assistants. Angel, do you take the challenge?"

Angel was the only bald eagle that had proved to be faster than Chief Rushing Wind in their dive-and-grab contests. She had earned the respect of all, including the Chief who was not one bit jealous of his beautiful granddaughter. She had many suitors but had not chosen one yet, waiting for the Supreme-Eagle-in-the-Sky to say, "This is the one." All agreed she was the one to assume the task.

Angel straightened her wings and replied, "Chief and family, I am more than willing to take the challenge. I'll do it right now even in the daylight."

"Of course! Of course!" They all chorused enthusiastically.

The forest below heard the chorus and became excited and somewhat fearful. A bear suggested it must be wind in the treetops, which they all decided was reasonable and went to their homes since it was lunchtime followed by siestas.

Angel took off heading for the ripe wild fig trees, a favorite for squirrels, mentally strategizing as she flew. She scattered some woodpeckers temporarily until they realized she was not a threat. She plucked a large fig leaf and wrapped two figs in it. She then flew silently to an oak tree where she picked two acorns and placed them in the fig leaf bundle. Angel positioned herself on a lower tree branch just a few feet above Ragged's cell ready for the drop. She sat quietly for a few moments wondering how she could make her presence known without scaring him, since he was the excitable type and might scream. She aimed an acorn perfectly at one of the spaces between the roof branches. It fell right in front of Ragged causing him to grab it immediately and then look up. The next acorn nearly missed his nose. He dove for the second acorn and stuffed both in his cheeks as quickly as he could. As soon as Angel felt it was safe, she flew silently down to the front of the jail cell where Ragged could see her. On landing, she tossed a fig into the cell. Ragged's mouth was full, so he was unable to emit any sound despite his fear.

Angel immediately whispered, "Ragged, we are planning to rescue you, but we need to time this perfectly so you will not be missed for a while. Just keep very quiet, even if your rescue gets scary. OK?" Ragged nodded with his cheeks still full. Angel rolled the remaining fig into the cell. "I'll be back soon, so be ready," she murmured as she took off. She was amazed at his flimsy cell, at how easy the rescue would be and wondered why he had not attempted an escape. "I suppose he's frozen with fear," she mused. She thought of rescuing him right then by herself but dismissed it,

since his cage was exposed to view and was in the bright sunlight.

In the meantime, the entire Tribe counseled with the Supreme-Eagle-in-the-Sky for the rescue and abduction strategies. Angel chose four swift and silent eagles, Clear Water, Thunder, Straight

Arrow and White Cloud, who

To the Rescue!

began methodically practicing the instructions in pantomime.

That night they descended one at a time into the trees above the jail cell. The four eagles on cue from Angel slipped stealthily to the jail roof and told Ragged, "Don't move a muscle!" They silently untied the corner branches and removed the roof. The warning for Ragged not to move was unnecessary, since he could only shake with fear. Thunder motioned to Ragged to look up as Angel swept down from the overhead branch, scooped him up and whisked him away so rapidly that he fainted.

Angel flew Ragged to her eyrie, where several gathered to watch over him. When Ragged revived, he was welcomed, told he was safe and was asked for his address. Straight Arrow intervened, "Perhaps we should not return him to his home right away since they know where he lives, and that will be the first place they look." Ragged Tail was given more seeds and figs.

Angel had charge over the abduction of President Fox. She recruited seven more to divert the guards at the president's entrance and escape routes. Twice a week at midnight, President Fox received his delivery of contraband duck by two well-armed and still loyal Secret Service Raccoons. At those predicted times the president would emerge from his hole, stretch, and wait for the Secret Service. Angel timed the dive-and-grab right before the delivery was in sight. Confusion and fear reigned when the guards saw the eagles, and the abduction was flawless. The terrified duck escaped without injuries and with thankful quacks.

President S. Fox was taken to an abandoned, reinforced, and inescapable eyrie. The president was afraid of heights and could not peer over the edge. All the eagles gathered around giving thanks to the Supreme-Eagle-in-the-Sky and celebrating boisterously, further alarming the forest citizens below.

• •

An Imperfect Metaphor

The Supreme-Eagle-in-the-Sky is a simile for our Heavenly Father Who knows all and sees all. However, a metaphor always has limitations in that only the most important comparisons apply. He represents a source of wisdom and guidance but not all the supernatural attributes of our matchless Father God in heaven. Cultures typically imagine God as a similar image to them, just as the eagles understood theirs as an eagle. Our conception about our Creator also tends to be inaccurate and too small. He is infinitely greater than the created.

Paralysis

Fear can be paralyzing. An outstanding example in Scripture of the damage fear caused is the Old Testament story of the twelve spies assigned to scope out the Promised Land for the Israelites before they entered (Numbers 13-14). The spies returned with evidence of the great abundance in the land—one grape cluster hung on a pole requiring two men to carry it—along with the report of giants in the land. Ten of the twelve spies were fearful, considering themselves grasshoppers compared with the giants. Only two men, Joshua and Caleb, full of faith in God's ability to perform His Word, reported they were well able to take the land because God was with them. The ten negative reports caused the majority of the congregation to complain, wail and want to return to slavery in Egypt. God called the negative reports evil, due to their unbelief and fear. The result— forty years wasted in the desert, the same footsteps traveled year after year with funerals held for the fearful who did not believe what God had said. He would permit only the faithful to enter the Promised Land.

Fear is is one of Satan's weapons. Has fear ever attacked you? Did you freeze when asked to give an answer in class? Did you quake for hours before an assignment in speech class? Has someone threatened you with road rage? A plethora of fears have interesting labels such as the following most common phobias:[1]

— spiders: arachnophobia
— strangers: xenophobia
— heights: acrophobia
— open spaces: agoraphobia
— small spaces: claustrophobia

---

1. *The World Book Encyclopedia.* 1991. s.v. "Phobia." 391.

You name an object and there might be an official phobia name for it. Many phobias on a lengthy list are astonishing, such as a label for the fear of 666! The extensive list highlights the seriousness of fears that are true bondages for some folks. Many situations definitely warrant fear such as fire, but if unreasonable fears control your life, you must eventually deal with them or never be free. The answer to overcoming permanently is usually beyond human ability.

The Antidote

What will counteract fear? Grace, faith and love (1 John 4:18) are stronger than fear. Grace and faith are the undeserved gifts from God that enable us to be courageous and to love with His love through His infinite mercy (Ephesians 2:4-10).

Faith in self is misplaced because it is often shaken by emotions. Personality or education is quaky ground on which to build faith— remember human beings are faulty and finite—not omniscient (knowing all) like God. The eagles sought wisdom beyond their experience to overcome fear and to receive perfect strategies.

Fear first entered humanity through Satan's deception that we could rule selves as little gods, resulting in the expulsion from God's presence. With fear came the universal doubt that God loves us.

The only sure foundation for faith and love is the Lord Jesus Christ, the Messiah and His Word. Faith comes when we hear the Word of God (Romans 10:17). Countless stories report someone singing a Christian hymn or quoting Scripture to overcome mass fear. The next time you experience fear, do that—sing a hymn or quote a Scripture to yourself audibly. You may have to repeat it a few times to override fear but faith will kick in. A reminder—Psalm 103:20 states God's holy angels listen for us to speak the Word of God that sets them in motion to bring it to pass. You will be amazed by the power of the Word.

Added Blessing

Peace accompanies grace, faith, mercy and love in conquering fear. Psalm 91 contains the Lord's promises of long life, deliverance from sickness and terrorism and more. Even though God's love is not stated specifically in this Psalm, it is evident in the provisions promised for those who will believe and come into His presence—His "secret place." It is a priceless resource to memorize. Quote the entire psalm any time you feel fearful about anything, or carry a copy with you if needed. Anytime I am around someone sick, I *speak* verses six and ten as a reminder to myself and to the Lord as a declaration of my dependence on Him. God's Word works every time!

The verses are not good luck charms. They are the Lord's power waiting for us to believe that He is Who He says He is and He will do what He says He will do. It is impossible for God to lie (Titus 1:2; Numbers 23:19) because He is 100 percent truth and holiness.

Moral Of The Story
— *Practical lesson:* Remember, fear and faith are opposites.
— *Spiritual lesson:* Let the Word of God bring grace to fight and conquer fear.

What other lessons might be contained here?

Victory From Above

When you need help, look up.

President S. Fox was scared out of his skin but faked boldness. After all, a president must act presidential in all situations. The few still loyal weasels not sentenced to house arrest and all the remaining Badger Militia were so confused that they left the jail cells

Party Animals

and ghettos unguarded, were too ashamed to return to their families and went into hiding. The Raccoon Secret Service had already defected.

At dawn, the president's absence was noticed. A search began until one of the hiding badgers that had guarded the duck delivery was discovered and told all. Good news traveled like a grapevine on steroids and the forest citizens began to party. Bears and rabbits danced, coyotes and wolves howled, birds chirped, mountain lions screeched and moose bellowed. The noise shook the trees and made the ghetto residents quake with fear, not knowing what had transpired.

The eagles landed silently and out of sight in the trees to observe. Attempting to restore order was futile, so they simply watched until the citizens wore themselves out and went home happy. The bears had eaten so many berries they were groaning. The eagles went back to their eyries to rest and to seek counsel again with the Supreme-Eagle-in-the-Sky. President Fox was on an emotional roller coaster of dejection, anger and fear, worrying about his future and already thinking about relocating to another forest.

One of the braver beavers volunteered to deliver the message to the ghettos, "Fve havf ven ththet vvree! Prethidentf Foxf isf gone! No one knowthstf vfere!" Miraculously, all deciphered. Cheers went up from the porcupines causing quills to shoot at random with every joy jiggle. The quills were immediately gathered and hidden just in case. Fortunately, the venomous snakes' ranks had been drastically thinned by infighting and by eagles and hawks, because they were sneaking across the ghetto borders. At the first sight of a venomous snake, a bobcat loudly screeched a warning for the entire forest to be on the lookout again.

Reverend Bright Morning Eagle checked on President Fox in an attempt to minister to him and to bring him a mouse for breakfast. The president's eyes lit up at the sight of the mouse, then tried to hide his reaction by fretting, muttering and feigning disdain. He quickly realized all regulations would be thrown out the proverbial window, so he decided to enjoy breakfast. It was his first experience at truthfulness. He set aside his worries for later.

The forest began to stir late the following morning. Happy, yawning faces greeted each other. The bears were more gassy than usual, and everyone shouted at them to get lost. Many questions remained unanswered and no one knew what to do next. One of the coyotes arrested for regulations violations leaked the news that President S. Fox's first name is Sly. The president had never mentioned a first name and no one had asked. The citizens began to realize they had been dumb. They had needed truth but they got outright lies and twisted subjective truth. Horatio Hawk suggested that a meeting was in order to reverse the unfair regulations, to fire all Badger Militia, Weasel Tax Collectors and Raccoon Secret Service and dismantle the jail cells. All cheered.

Chief Rushing Wind learned Horatio Hawk was gathering citizens to himself to influence their decisions. The Chief knew Horatio personally and voiced his concern that the forest was too vulnerable at this point to choose another leader who might be a repeat of President Fox. He proposed to all the eagles the time might be right to introduce themselves to the forest residents and return Ragged Tail to the forest floor.

Reverend Bright Morning was the first to speak, "Chief, I do believe we have the advantage because of our connection to the Supreme-Eagle-in-the-Sky. We need to ask our source for wisdom and a strategy to bring truth and restoration to our beloved forest."

Straight Arrow responded, "That is wisdom speaking right there." All eagles agreed, so immediately all began to reverently request guidance from the Supreme-Eagle-in-the-Sky.

During this quiet time a message from the Mountain Bald Eagle Tribe came to the Chief, delivered by a handsome eagle named Quick Silver. "We've been seeking the Supreme-Eagle-in-the-Sky on your behalf, so our tribe would now like to meet with you. We are also aware of the difficulties you are dealing with and offer our assistance."

The Forest Tribe all rejoiced again sending more echoes to the puzzled and fearful forest inhabitants below. Chief Rushing Wind spoke with enthusiasm and humility, "We gratefully welcome your assistance! Please come as soon as possible." Quick Silver took flight like Mercury with the message from the Chief and sending a little thrill through Angel's heart.

Within three hours, the Mountain Bald Eagle Tribe's chief and warriors arrived and landed in the treetops. After introductions all around, they discussed many strategies. Mountain Chief White Water stated, "This won't be difficult. We have the advantage of surprise and numbers—and, of course, our blessings from the Supreme-Eagle-in-the-Sky." Both tribes began rejoicing and were not quiet, causing the forest inhabitants to all quake, quickly gather their families and scurry into their nests, burrows, and dens.

"Yes." They all chorused. "Are we ready?" All nodded.

Chief Rushing Wind thunderously shouted, "Now!" Both tribes swooped to the ground at once.

The first citizen to catch sight of the eagles was a crow that screeched at the highest volume alerting all the forest. Heads popping up from burrows wide-eyed with fear saw what they thought were prehistoric extinct creatures. Few creatures other than snakes and hawks had seen an eagle for dozens of years.

"We have your President Fox in a safe place," announced Chief Rushing Wind. "We've been observing deterioration of the forest for several years, and we know exactly what the trouble is and have some suggestions for you."

"We now know what the trouble is," spoke Horatio, "and we're thankful that Sly Fox is out. That's why I've been trying to organize enough residents to change things here."

The Chief diplomatically interrupted, "Certainly things need to change, but we must be very careful how it is done and who does it. Everyone must realize by now that putting one individual in charge is a dangerous idea. Our Forest and Mountain Bald Eagle Tribes are organized, but we have all taken an oath to be submitted to the Supreme-Eagle-in-the-Sky. We have councils to make decisions only after seeking wisdom from this source. I would advise you to do the same."

"But, we don't know this Supreme-Eagle-in-the-Sky," piped up the largest Jack Rabbit.

"We can introduce him to you. In fact, we need to introduce ourselves to you. We are not dinosaurs. I'm Chief Rushing Wind of the Forest Bald Eagle Tribe, and this is Chief White Water of the Mountain Bald Eagle Tribe. We've come to help. We joined to bring sanity to the forest. We live at the top of the tallest trees here, so you probably have not seen us for years."

Chief White Water declared, "Because our source of wisdom is the Supreme-Eagle-in-the-Sky, our tribes have survived and are strong through his guidance. We will be your council to suggest strategies from him if you agree. We truly believe you should accept our assistance, but it is up to you."

"Yes," interjected Chief Rushing Wind, "the decision is entirely yours. We will not force our solutions or suggestions on you but will seek your cooperation on every detail. You already agree that the forest is a mess, and you haven't many clues about how to correct it. We want you to vote soon on whether or not to let us assist you. What do you say?"

Horatio Hawk defiantly exclaimed, "What right have to you to interfere or tell us what to do? You've not been part of us. And your Supreme Eagle has nothing to do with us either."

Angel arose in defense, "Oh, quite the contrary! We are very much a part of your society and we care about this forest. You just have not been aware of us because of the heights of our dwellings and the fact that we don't need or even want recognition. You just haven't seen or heard of some of the rescues we've done for the dwellers on the outskirts of your dysfunctional community, because most of those that have been rescued are embarrassed." Angel's eyes sought out Quick Silver who was admiring her beauty and gracious words. He made the decision to learn more about her.

The community decided to make peace with and to encourage the badgers, weasels and raccoons to rejoin the forest in unity. Some were still in hiding, unable to believe they would ever be forgiven and accepted again. The citizens who showed up to vote were in 100 percent agreement to accept help from the bald eagle tribes.

• • • • •

From that point, the forest began its progress toward normalcy. All illogical regulations were canceled, jails dismantled, all fences and barricades at the ghetto borders above and below ground removed and apartment tree nests separated. Beavers were allowed to dam the channel to the gardens and return to their way of life. Sly was evicted from his plush, roomy den, which was quickly converted to a meeting hall and assistance center for the displaced and needy.

A just punishment for the ex-president had not been decided, so he remained in the eyrie under guard. Heated debates stretched indecision to many days and meetings. Some insisted on hanging him for treason while others were softer and believed house arrest in a hollow tree with limited perimeter access would be sufficient. Most agreed Sly would be challenged even if he could repent and change. Hardliners also maintained emphatically that the badgers, raccoons and weasels who had taken the greatest delight in tormenting inmates be punished along with the ex-president, perhaps be incarcerated. Old thinking patterns stalled any decisions, and friendships were nearly broken in the process. Both Eagle Tribes intervened.

Chief Rushing Wind suggested, "Let's simply ignore Sly. Just don't pay any attention to his words or presence at all. That may impress him the most since he's really quite social. Perhaps he'll begin to see the errors of his ways. This way gives him a chance to repent and change. If that doesn't work, we could at least hope he'll find another forest. Treason is a serious thing, and it's a good idea to institute a strategy to deal with it in the future. Sly Fox isn't the only one who lusts after power." The Chief's eyes drifted toward Horatio Hawk. Several noticed and nodded.

"Well-spoken," commented an anti-Fox badger. This appears to be the easiest and best solution to this mess." The rest who were weary of this ordeal whistled and cheered in agreement.

"All right then," stated the Chief. "It's settled. We'll release Sly immediately and warn him about what to expect from the citizens. He'll also know we'll be watching him closely. And, if he decides to move to another forest, we'll send a warning to his new location ahead of or after him."

The citizens were so energized by the improvements that they began to inquire about the Supreme-Eagle-in-the-Sky. Reverend Bright Morning set up teaching sessions in the assistance center for all who wished to attend.

Trouble reared its head again and peace in the forest vanished. A small number objected to the use of a public place for religious instruction and boldly picketed the assistance center with demands that all classes cease immediately.

An impressive buck and his small entourage that had always remained silent but were keen observers of the cultural and political atmospheres, found courage to speak for the first time. "You protesters can easily find another place for your platforms. There's plenty of room in the forest for diversity. Not everyone has to think or believe the same thing here," he reasoned. "I would think by now everyone would understand Bishop Owl's stance was an incorrect understanding of tolerance. We have freedom of choice now."

Many cheered. The Eagle chiefs and warriors were exceedingly pleased that a group of forest citizens brought correction without prompting from the eagles and joined the cheering. Chief Rushing Wind suggested taking a vote on this issue to lay it to rest. More cheering. The poll revealed only two percent supported the protest, eighteen percent were undecided and eighty percent were in favor of continuing the assistance center instruction. The protesters unashamedly stomped away.

· · · · ·

Mutual admiration was growing between Quick Silver and Angel. Quick Silver felt slightly intimidated when he learned Angel was Chief Rushing Wind's granddaughter, but was more impressed when he learned of her abilities and achievements. They began spending much time together and had learned to trust each other. Both tribes were well aware of their smitten condition and did what they could to encourage and not interfere. Quick Silver mustered the gumption to ask Chief Rushing Wind if he could offer the Pure White Rabbit to Angel.

Heart beating nearly out of his chest, he approached the Chief who was prepared for his visit.

"You have a request?" preempted the Chief before Quick Silver could open his mouth.

"Uh, yes sir. Uh, I want, uh, your permission to, uh, offer the Pure-White-Rabbit-to-Angel." His last few words spilled out so quickly that they were nearly unintelligible.

"What will you do if she refuses the offer?" teased the Chief.

Quick Silver had not considered that possibility, believing asking the Chief would be his greatest challenge. "Uh, I don't know, sir," was his shaky reply. "Uh, I don't think I could live without her."

"Well, my goodness, son. Be at peace. You have my permission to present the offering to her. Have you two discussed this?"

"No sir, not directly, but..."

"Go on," interjected the Chief with twinkling eyes and wave of a wing. "Just let me know when you plan to do this."

"Oh, yes sir! I must construct the carrier and go hunting right now!" Eagerness was written all over him.

Angel began to worry about not seeing or hearing from Quick Silver. She took her concerns to the Chief whose response gave her no hint of the reason for his absence. "I don't see any need for worry. He's on an errand and is well able to take care of himself."

"But he didn't tell me he was going anywhere," she complained, worrying about what she thought was a growing relationship and hoping she had not hoped too much.

After two weeks, Quick Silver was ready and contacted Chiefs Rushing Wind and White Water. The Chiefs called both the forest and mountain citizens to come to the assistance center. All came except most of the rabbits that misunderstood and were afraid of being chosen for this event. Those who ventured to attend remained out of sight just in case. Nearly all forest residents attended along with many of the mountain residents. Noticeably present was Mr. Ragged Tail, who, upon returning to earth, found instant celebrity status as Braveheart with dedicated fans hanging onto every exaggerated word of his ordeal.

Everyone except Angel knew the purpose for gathering, and secret keeping skills were tested to the max. No one spoke despite big grins, muffled giggles, dancing and hyper-excitement. Angel did not question the oversized crowd. Her usual keen observation skills had been diverted to concern about Quick Silver's location. She looked for him in the crowd but did not see him, adding to her agitation and concern.

Quick Silver suddenly swooped down unannounced from the trees at the edge of the crowd and startled the citizens hovering close by. They quickly composed themselves to continue the secret. Quick Silver's claws clutched a small carrier built of branches artistically decorated with wild grapevine leaves. The Pure White Rabbit peered from the cage with wide, frightened eyes. When the few brave rabbits present saw Quick Silver arrive with the gift for Angel, they sent word to the rest that they were all safe and not to miss this extraordinary and exciting event. Quick Silver flew to a tree directly above Angel without her notice due to her eyes still searching for him among the crowd. He appeared in the air and stood before her with his gift. Nearly overcome with emotion, he asked Angel in a shaky voice, "Will you receive the Pure White Rabbit?" Angel was stunned for only a moment, and then

responded with a strong "Yes!" Exuberant rejoicing could be heard for miles.

The Wedding

• •

Outcomes

Do you wish all life would turn out as well as this story? Numerous unhappy turns in human experiences defy understanding and tempt us to question God's goodness. Bad things do happen to good folks and good things to the unrighteous. Knowing the reasons might be delayed or remain a mystery. Personal bad choices can result in hardship or even disaster, and evil exists that people often have no personal responsibility in causing. Never forget Satan is a bad dude, the author of all evil, and he will do everything he can to mess up lives. Whatever the cause, God teaches lessons in all events, and we should be prepared for the bitter truth if we are culpable.

When we stay close to the Lord, He will guide us into all truth (John 8:31-32). Listen carefully because He promised the Holy Spirit would reveal truth to us (John 16:33). We cannot control all events in our lives, but we can be led by the Lord through and from situations with lessons learned. The matter of having control will be addressed again in detail in the sequel to this book. God also promised to turn all things around for good (Romans 8:28).

The Importance of Being Thankful

Thanking God and praising Him fulfills one of the reasons we are created. His asking for our praise and worship is not from a need for ego strokes, but just to acknowledge His existence. Praising and thanking God for Who He is and what He can do opens our hearts and minds to receive from Him—quite mysterious but true. It is His way of blessing us. Prayer, praise, worship and believing His Word are invitations allowing Him to mature us. He never makes a forced entry and will come when invited.

The Right Response to Evil

A gripping story in Acts 16:16-40 demonstrates praise and worship opening the way for a miracle. Paul and Silas had gone to Philippi to preach the Gospel. A young slave girl possessed by a divination spirit followed them and was making a good living for her owners. She stated repeatedly, "These men are servants of the Most High God." She was speaking truth, but from the wrong spirit, and Paul wanted his message disassociated from the enemy. Paul cast the demon out of her, and her owners were livid, because she could no longer earn money for them. They had Paul and Silas thrown into prison where they were severely beaten and locked in stocks. Paul and Silas did not complain, question why or accuse God of mistreating them. Instead, they began singing praises loudly so that all the inmates heard them. God rescued them with an earthquake to loosen their stocks that also unlocked all jail cells. Paul and Silas were released, and the jailer with his household accepted the Lord for salvation. See what praise and thanksgiving can do?

> 16 Rejoice always,
> 17 pray without ceasing,
> 18 in everything give thanks; for this is the will of God in
>   Christ Jesus for you (1 Thessalonians 5:16-18).

We need the Holy Spirit's power to obey the above verses. Notice thanksgiving and praise are not necessarily *for* every circumstance. Some events are just evil such as child molestation and more. We give thanksgiving and praise *in* everything, because God will be invited to do His will when Scripture is believed and implemented. The God of Abraham, Isaac and Jacob (the Father, the Son Jesus and the Holy Spirit) can do anything. Nothing is too hard for Him (Jeremiah 32:17; Matthew 19:26). God is still in the business of destroying the works of evil through our cooperation. Surrendering everything to Him gives Him your permission to intervene on your behalf. It is always your choice. He will not barge in uninvited. Again, after the ordeal, you will understand why you can thank Him *for* everything—with valuable lessons learned.

Moral Of The Story
— *Practical lesson:* Affliction can cleanse or make us bitter depending upon our choice.
— *Spiritual lesson:* Take First Thessalonians 5:16-18 to heart to be a winner in and over circumstances.

What other lessons might be contained in this parable?

Appendix

Contour Iris

About the Author/Illustrator

Diane Shields Spears lives in Texas with her husband, Truman, since 1977, has a B.A. in art, English and education, an M. A. in Christian counseling and an Ed. D. in Christian education. Diane is all level Texas state certified and has been an educator off-and-on since 1964 in both public and private school settings.

Her last public assignment was with Edgewood I.S.D., San Antonio, Texas, as the Fine Arts Curriculum Specialist-Coordinator, and during her last year, Head of Visual Arts and full time art instructor for the Edgewood Academy of Fine Arts. Other settings include home and private schools in grades five to eight core curriculum, K-8 music, and K-12 art.

Diane is now retired and continues drawing, painting, writing curriculum, poetry, and prose. She has taught all ages Sunday school classes, children's church and has served in various other church activities.

Diane has a background of personal achievement in the art world including featured artist exhibits, first place cash awards, free-lance commercial illustrations, illustrating children's activity books and is represented in many private art collections.

Spears Art Studio Christian Art Curricula

Diane has authored several Bible based art instruction manuals used in many educational settings:

— home school families and co-ops
— private Christian schools
— independent study
— missionaries

— vacation Bible schools
— public school art teachers as supplementary materials.

Spears Art Studio Mission Statement

1. to recognize God's Word and His hand in everything and to give Him glory;
2. to reconnect the Lord as the Supreme Artist into the process and excitement of art for both children and educators;
3. to provide resources for the Christian educator that:
   a. help students make connections between the Creator, creativity and personal maturity;
   b. are organized for natural learning progression;
   c. provide experiences for higher order thinking skills;
   e. "stretch" academic and manipulative skills;
   f. introduce students to famous artists and artworks in a seasonal and/or art elements/principles arrangement of art and craft production.

Spears Art Studio art curriculum manuals relate God's Word, art history, and art appreciation to specific themes and to each art activity within those themes. Students use a variety of art materials, learn many techniques in art production, and grow in their ability for expression and appreciation of art. All curricula are adaptable to any study schedule and are non-consumable due to the limited reproduction rights notice in each curriculum and on the web site.

— *Spears Art Studio K-8 Christian Art Curriculum, a Teacher's Manual©* is primarily organized according to seasons, with several other major themes interspersed throughout. Each activity is appropriate for grade and age abilities, and builds toward the next level in brain and motor skills with a wealth of activity choices. The curriculum has the potential to cover nine years of art instruction with many extra choices and uses common items students already have and some items normally found in the home.

— *Spears Art Studio High School Art Survey ©,* a student manual, is a beginning art course for students at any high school grade level, is an Art 1 equivalent with an accreditation option and supports the Classical Christian Education model.

The areas of study cover the major art elements and principles through drawing, painting, three-dimension, graphics, and varied media.

— *Spears Art Studio Beginning Calligraphy Workbook for Grade Five Through Adult* © contains simple directions with tracing pages.

All curriculum pages are reproducible following the Limited Copyright instructions posted on the web site and on the copyright page of each manual.

All products of Spears Art Studio, Inc. are dedicated to the glory of our Lord and Savior Jesus Christ of Nazareth.

Please visit http://www.spearsartstudio.com
— free curricula downloads
— original fine art

Printed in the United States
By Bookmasters